▲▲▲▲▲▲▲▲▲▲▲▲▲▲▲▲▲▲▲▲▲▲▲▲▲▲▲▲▲▲▲▲▲▲▲▲▲

L I F E W A Y S

The *Pueblo*

R A Y M O N D   B I A L

▼▼▼▼▼▼▼▼▼▼▼▼▼▼▼▼▼▼▼▼▼▼▼▼▼▼▼▼▼▼▼▼▼▼▼▼▼

BENCHMARK BOOKS

MARSHALL CAVENDISH
NEW YORK

SERIES CONSULTANT: JOHN BIERHORST

ACKNOWLEDGMENTS

This book would not have been possible without the gracious assistance of a number of individuals and organizations, including many native people, who have devoted themselves to sustaining the traditions and enriching the contemporary life of the Pueblos. I am especially indebted to Joe Sando and Pat Reck at the Pueblo Cultural Center for their guidance and kind permission to photograph at the museum. I would also like to thank the fine people at Pueblo de San Ildefonso for allowing me to take photographs in their lovely community. I would like to acknowledge Ray Martinez, manager of Babbitt's Cottonwood Trading Post, for his wonderful hospitality. I would also like to acknowledge the assistance of the University of New Mexico Archives, the Northern Arizona University Archives, the National Archives, the Library of Congress, and the Philbrook Museum of Art for furnishing a number of illustrations.

I would like to express my deep appreciation to my editor, Kate Nunn, and to Doug Sanders at Marshall Cavendish for their tremendous encouragement and hard work in refining *The Pueblo* and other titles in the Lifeways series. I am also very much indebted to John Bierhorst for his many careful corrections and thoughtful suggestions. As always, I would like to thank my wife, Linda, and my children, Anna, Sarah, and Luke for their support. It was especially wonderful to go on the photo assignment in the company of Linda, Sarah, and Luke, and then to complete the research and writing of this book in the midst of my family back at home.

Benchmark Books
Marshall Cavendish Corporation
99 White Plains Road Tarrytown, New York 10591-9001
Text copyright © 2000 by Raymond Bial
Illustration copyright © 2000 by the Marshall Cavendish Corporation
Map by Rodica Prato
All rights reserved. No part of this book may be reproduced in any form without
written permission from the publisher.
Library of Congress Cataloging-in-Publication Data
Bial, Raymond.
The Pueblo / Raymond Bial.
p. cm. — (Lifeways)
Includes bibliographical references and index.
Summary: Discusses the history, culture, beliefs, changing ways,
and notable people of the Pueblo.
ISBN 0-7614-0861-4 (lib. bdg.)
1. Pueblo Indians–History–Juvenile literature. 2. Pueblo Indians–Material culture–Juvenile literature. 3.
Pueblo Indians–Social life and customs–Juvenile literature. [1. Pueblo Indians. 2. Indians of North
America–Southwest, New.] I.Title
II. Series: Bial, Raymond. Lifeways.
E99.P9B453   2000
978.9'004974–dc21   98-48299
CIP   AC
Printed in Italy
6 5 4

Cover photos by Raymond Bial

The photographs in this book are used by permission and through the courtesy of: The Philbrook Museum of Art, Tulsa, Oklahoma: 1, 15, 35, 53, 54, 57, 86. Raymond Bial: 6, 8-9, 12, 17, 23, 25, 26-27, 31, 36 (bottom), 40-41, 61 (top), 66, 69, 80-81, 83, 84, 88-89, 98-99, 100-101, 103, 104, 108-109. Northern Arizona University, Cline Library, Special Collections & Archives: 11, 91. Amon Carter Museums, Fort Worth, Texas: Frederick Inman Monsen, *[Overview of Indian pueblo riding high atop mesa]*, ca. 1900, toned gelatin silver print, P1991.12.5, 24; Richard H. Kern, *Women Grinding Corn*, 1852, tones lithograph, 1976.69.6, 36 (top); Howard Norton Cook, *Taos Pueblo, Moonlight*, 1927, woodcut, 1997.39, 107. National Archive: 29, 67. University of New Mexico, Center for Southwest Research: neg. no. 000-478-4274, 43; neg. no. 000-099-0538, 45; neg. no. 994-045-0020, 47; neg. no. 994-045-0019, 50; neg. no. 000-494-1403, 75; neg. no. 000-009-0286, 85; neg. no. 000-332-0474, 95; neg. no. 000-093-0016, 112; neg. no. 996-030-0006, 113 & 114; neg. no. 000-478-0192, 118. Museum of New Mexico: neg. no. 47480, 116.

This book is respectfully dedicated
to the Pueblo people, who have much
to teach us about ourselves and
our place in the universe.

Contents

Author's Note

AT THE DAWN OF THE TWENTIETH CENTURY, NATIVE Americans were thought to be a vanishing race. However, despite four hundred years of warfare, deprivation, and disease, American Indians have not gone away. Countless thousands have lost their lives, but over the course of this century the populations of native tribes have grown tremendously. Even as American Indians struggle to adapt to modern Western life, they have also kept the flame of their traditions alive—the language, religion, stories, and the everyday ways of life. An exhilarating renaissance in Native American culture is now sweeping the nation from coast to coast.

The *Lifeways* books depict the social and cultural life of the major nations, from the early history of native peoples in North America to their present-day struggles for survival and dignity. Historical and contemporary photographs of traditional subjects, as well as period illustrations, are blended throughout each book so that readers may gain a sense of family life in a tipi, a hogan, or a longhouse.

No single book can comprehensively portray the intricate and varied lifeways of an entire tribe, or nation. I only hope that young people will come away with a deeper appreciation for the rich tapestry of Indian culture—both then and now—and a keen desire to learn more about these first Americans.

1. Origins

The story of the Pueblo cannot be told without an understanding of their abiding relationship with the land—stunning expanses of parched deserts and high mountains.

OVER A CENTURY AGO, THE EXPLORER AND PHOTOGRAPHER WILLIAM Henry Jackson made his way up the side of a canyon in what would one day become Mesa Verde National Park. Seven hundred feet up, Jackson stumbled upon houses tucked into the canyon walls—an entire village made of stone, timber, and mud bricks called adobe. Now celebrated as Cliff Palace Pueblo, the abandoned village was one of many awaiting discovery at Mesa Verde, Chaco Canyon, Canyon de Chelly (shay), and other locations scattered throughout the American Southwest in the present states of Arizona, Utah, Colorado, and New Mexico. Although long abandoned, the villages clearly showed that a great civilization of early Pueblo people had once lived there. They were called the Anasazi, which means "the ancient enemies" or "the ancient strangers" in Navajo. Today, most experts translate the word simply as "the ancient ones."

The Anasazi, whose town-building civilization dates from about A.D. 700, had no written language, and today no one is certain what they called themselves. Their ruined settlements have been given Spanish and English names. Although there are many unanswered questions about their way of life, it is clear that they developed an elaborate civilization and left an important legacy to their descendants—the Pueblo people of today. Pueblo, which means "town" in Spanish, is the name by which the Anasazi have been most commonly known. They were the only native peoples north of Mexico who lived in clusters of rectangular stone buildings, often in large apartment houses, and who spun and wove cotton into garments.

*C*haco Canyon was once home to thousands of Anasazi people. One of the larger cities there was Pueblo Bonito, or Beautiful Village, which had hundreds of rooms and kivas.

The Pueblos have never been one people. They spoke—and still speak—several distinct languages, which include many dialects. Among the Pueblo groups are the Hopi, or "peaceful ones," living in eight or nine villages on the mesas of northeastern Arizona and the neighboring Zuñi, who live in six or seven villages lying just over the border in New Mexico. Over the centuries, the Hopis and Zuñis have often visited each other and shared many customs. Today, they are considered the western or desert Pueblos. Living far away in villages along the fertile valley of the Rio Grande in present-day New Mexico are the eastern or

As seen at San Ildefonso, people continue to make their homes in the old way—with timber frames covered by adobe. The thick clay walls of these houses remain cool in the summer and warm in the winter.

river Pueblos: the Taos, Tiwa (TEE-wa), Tewa (TAY-wa), and Towa peoples. In between are the remaining Keres, who live at Laguna and at Acoma.

Yet these groups, each with its own language and traditions, follow similar ways of life. They share styles of housing, clothing, artistry, and religion. The Pueblos have traditionally been resourceful people, planting corn, cotton, tobacco, squash, beans, and sunflower seeds. Unlike other native peoples whose women undertook most of the tedious labor, the men too worked in the fields. For hundreds of years, the Pueblos have woven colorful garments, shaped lovely pottery, and created remarkable jewelry. And they have held rain dances in blazes of color, adorned with their jewelry, feathers, and capes.

With a population of around 20,000 people, the early Pueblos lived in an area of about four and half million acres. According to traditional history, the first people emerged from beneath the surface of the earth. Up they came from the *sipapu*, or "navel of the world," which is today represented by the hole in the floor of the kiva (KEE-vuh), a sacred chamber where rituals are held. Over the years the kivas have changed in size and shape, but no village is without one. According to some versions of the story, the people surfaced from a lake. Here is a version of the story about how the Pueblos came to their homeland told by the Tewa people of the Rio Grande:

"The Emergence Story"

Long ago, the people lived under the surface of a great lake. Nearby lived the spirit beings and the animals. Two of the spirit beings, Corn Mother Close-to-Summer and Corn Mother Close-to-Winter, asked if anyone would be willing to lead the people out of the water. They had to ask four times before one man, who became the Hunt Chief, stepped forward.

Rising to the next layer of water, the Hunt Chief came upon animals who were so frightened they scratched his skin over his entire body. However, they had not meant to harm him so they tended his wounds and presented him with a bow and arrow, an eagle feather for his hair, and mud to paint his face. The Hunt Chief returned to his people and he began to dance and sing before them.

The Corn Mothers praised his effort, but also said, "You will need other leaders to help you." Walking among the people, they gave an ear of blue corn to a man who became the Summer Leader. They presented an ear of white corn to another man who was named the Winter Leader. The Corn Mothers also assigned two helpers, called Towa é (Toh-wah AY), to these leaders, who went to the surface of the lake. At that time the people only knew two directions—above and below—and the Towa é threw handfuls of mud north, south, east, and west to create the four directions. Wherever the mud struck the earth, a mountain thrust upward and became a sacred home for the Tewa. Hunt Chief, Summer Leader, and Winter Leader then guided the people up from the lake.

The Winter and Summer Leaders assumed the places of the Corn Mothers, who continued to live below the water. They became known as Winter and Summer Mothers, or Little Mothers, although they were men. The earth was still too soft, so Summer Mother asked Winter Mother to go first. When Winter Mother placed a foot upon the earth, the ground froze hard, and the people began to journey south. As they traveled some of the

*C*orn Dancer, *a 1946 watercolor by San Ildefonso artist Louis Gonzales. The Pueblos revered corn, their most important food. The sacred grain represented prosperity.*

people became sick and unhappy, so the Mothers led them back into the lake and asked the Corn Mothers to help them. The Corn Mothers gave them the Medicine Society, along with medicine men to cure their illnesses, and the Clown Society to bring laughter into their hearts. The Winter and Summer Mothers had to return to the lake three more times: to bring forth a Hunt Society to provide the people with food, a War Society to defend themselves, and a Women's Society to empower women to heal and perform ceremonies.

When the people finally arrived at the Rio Grande, the Summer Mother turned to the western mountains and the people followed. The Winter Mother turned to the eastern mountains, and the people followed. After many years, all the people came together once again and built great villages in this place, which remains the home of the Pueblos to this very day.

LIKE OTHER NATIVE PEOPLES OF NORTH AMERICA, THE ANCESTORS OF the Pueblos were hunters and gatherers who made their way across the Bering Strait over a narrow land bridge that joined Asia and North America thousands of years ago. They may have come 12,000 years ago, but some scientists now think that Asian people migrated to North America between 28,000 and 38,000 years ago. During this Ice Age period, they hunted mammoths and giant bison along with deer and other small animals. The early Anasazi gradually wandered into what is now known as the Four Corners region of the Southwest. No one is certain when the Anasazi arrived or exactly where they came from. It is known that nomadic people were hunting with spears called atlatls and gathering wild seeds in the region thousands of years ago. Most likely, between 100 B.C. and A.D. 500, they settled in the northern part of the Southwest, living in caves or building rough shelters of poles and adobe. Dressed in animal skins and in skirts and sandals made from strips of yucca, they wove baskets for storing nuts and seeds, but had not yet learned to make clay pottery. They have been called the Basket Makers because of the many kinds of baskets found at their ruins—some so tightly woven they were used to hold water.

During this time the climate of the Southwest was cooler and wetter than it is today; there were sprawling grasslands and lines of trees along the riverbeds. The people formed a deep bond with the land that provided them with food, clothing, and shelter. They learned where to find water, stones for making weapons and tools, and wood for fires along with game and wild plants. As the land became more arid, they no longer wandered far from their homes, especially when they began to raise corn and other crops.

Adapted from a wild grass, corn had been grown in Mexico since about 4,000 B.C. Influenced by the Maya and other peoples living in Mexico and Central America, the early Anasazi first plant-

Men honed animal bones into sharp points and attached them to wooden shafts to make spears and arrows— deadly weapons for hunting and warfare.

ed the precious seeds around 1,500 years ago. They grew corn and squash to supplement their hunting and gathering of wild fruits, berries, seeds, and plants. They stored these foodstuffs in underground pits, often lined with stone slabs. It is also likely that they learned the art of pottery making and acquired many religious beliefs from their southern neighbors. Between A.D. 500 and 700, as the early Pueblos began to grow beans and cotton and raise turkeys, agriculture became more important than hunting and gathering.

Among the mesas and buttes, the Pueblos lived in underground dwellings called pit houses. Around A.D. 700 they began to build aboveground homes of stone and adobe, often connecting the structures. The pit houses came to be used as kivas, or ceremonial chambers, for rituals and as lodges for men. Kiva means "old house" in the Hopi language. During this period the Pueblos expanded their territory as far as central Utah and southern Colorado and throughout much of northern Mexico. Large numbers of people swarmed into the region and villages sprang up in desert country. Between 1050 and 1300, large pueblos were built in the recesses of canyon cliffs or high atop mesas. Resembling high-rise apartments, these cliff dwellings often had three, four, or five levels that seemed to be chiseled from the earth around them.

Anasazi civilization was centered in the Mesa Verde region in southwestern Colorado, the Chaco Canyon in northwestern New Mexico, and the Kayenta area of northeastern Arizona. Early

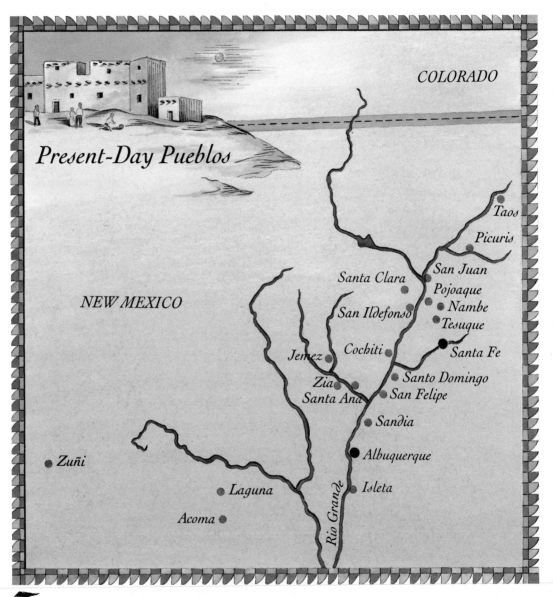

Present-Day Pueblos

COLORADO

NEW MEXICO

Taos

Picuris

Santa Clara

San Juan

Pojoaque

Nambe

San Ildefonso

Tesuque

Cochiti

Santa Fe

Jemez

Santo Domingo

Zia

San Felipe

Santa Ana

Sandia

Albuquerque

Zuñi

Isleta

Rio Grande

Laguna

Acoma

This map shows the present-day pueblos of New Mexico. Most of the pueblos are near the Rio Grande, which has historically been an important source of water. The Hopi live to the west in Arizona.

Pueblo people lived in cities, like Pueblo Bonito in Chaco Canyon, and in small villages; their ways were as different as city and country life are today. The people of Chaco Canyon were exceptional builders—Pueblo Bonito, which is Spanish for "beautiful village," has over eight hundred rooms and kivas. As many as five thousand people inhabited the Chaco Canyon area.

A large workforce also constructed a broad and intricate system of dirt roads, totaling more than four hundred miles, with five major thoroughfares. These roads were likely used for a sprawling trade network, the movement of workers, and religious processions. The Anasazi also used fires or sunlight reflected from mica mirrors to send messages from mesa tops. These flickering lights visible over great distances allowed outlying pueblos to communicate with each other. Chaco Canyon was also the site of other engineering wonders, including ingenious systems for diverting water to irrigate the fields and provide drinking water. Pueblo ancestors constructed stone dams to check water near streams and earthen dikes to slow runoff from rainstorms and snowmelt at the end of winter. A system of dams and dikes was also used to channel floodwaters onto their fields.

During this time the early Pueblos began to make pottery in a greater variety of shapes and styles, and they became skilled weavers. Growing into a sophisticated desert empire, the Pueblos flourished for about two hundred years in towns of stone and clay apartments in the plateau country and river valleys. They became well known and admired for their farming methods, building styles, and skill at adapting to new technologies and changing environments. Hundreds of years before Columbus arrived in North America they were living in great cities in the Southwest.

Then, just as miraculously as their culture had flowered, the Anasazi mysteriously disappeared—or so people once thought. Experts once speculated that a catastrophe had befallen the Anasazi—they had been overrun by barbarians or had outgrown their food supplies and died out. It was later believed that they suffered through years of drought, which prompted them to abandon the large towns and drift eastward to a more reliable source of water along the Rio Grande. Only the Hopi remained in their ancient homeland because they had the good fortune of living near springs that trickled precious water along the cliffs. However, it has since been proven that they had weathered previous droughts and that cities were abandoned before the onset of the dry years. Some scholars now think that the Anasazi may have been divided by religious controversy or were attracted to a new religion. In any case, the great cities declined, and the population shifted to the Rio Grande area of north-central New Mexico, where there are ruins at Aztec, Bandelier, and Pecos. Between 1300 and 1700 Pueblo ancestors also established the villages that are still inhabited today. Descendants of the Anasazi would face much hardship—fierce raids by the Apache and the Navajo and later, invasions by the Spanish and the Americans. Yet their life-ways have survived, and their culture shines brightly still in the desert sun.

The People and the Land

For thousands of years the Pueblos have lived in the vast, parched Southwest. It is a sprawling country of sage and cactus, of dazzling heights and relative depths. Silver threads of rivers have carved remarkable canyons deep into the rocky soul of this land. In the fertile valleys the Anasazi planted their fields of corn and cotton, forming blankets of vivid green against the rose and tan cliffs rising steeply on either side. On the lofty cliffs of Mesa Verde, Canyon de Chelly, and Chaco Canyon, the ancient ones built villages of rock and adobe. They have since forsaken these homes, but everywhere their spirits haunt the ruins.

Their Pueblo descendants now thrive in villages strung along the Rio Grande, or the Zuñi country of northwestern New Mexico. To the west in Arizona, the Hopis remain as always, amid the grandeur of the Painted Desert and the rolling country of pale green sage and yucca. Higher up, the plateaus are studded with emerald green piñon (PIN-yun), juniper, and rabbit bush. The land gradually rises to thick forests of pine and fir trees in the mountains. To the north and east is Taos Pueblo in the snow-capped mountains of northern New Mexico. Most of the Pueblos today are concentrated in the valley of the Rio Grande from the desert landscape surrounding Albuquerque to the high road north of Santa Fe. Wherever the Pueblos make their home, far in the distance are jagged mountain ranges topped with pure white snow through much of the year.

Sand covers the desert floor in shades of brown, from sun-bleached tan to rich chocolate. These flat lands are broken up by

The varied landscape of the Southwest includes parched deserts and snow-topped mountains. Here, the Anasazi and their descendants have lived for many generations.

tabletop mesas and high plateaus upon which some of the early Pueblos made their homes—as they still do today. Perched on a high mesa, Acoma is believed to be the oldest continuously inhabited village in North America. The distance is often streaked with mirages at the farthest edge of sight, while the sky overhead is either a rich, flawless blue or blooming with towering, ultra-white clouds.

*P*ueblos were sometimes built high atop mesas, seeming to hover between land and sky. Here, inhabitants have a breathtaking view of the desert, unfolding in all four directions to the distant horizon.

Many wild animals live in this varied geography, including lanky jackrabbits with large, scooping ears, tensely coiled rattlesnakes with ominously vibrating tails, and bristly peccaries, snorting and squealing as they scatter through dry creek beds called washes. And there is the wary coyote, always treading a thin line between people and wilderness. Mountain lions and bears make their home here, as well as deer, pronghorn antelope, and an occasional buffalo. To the Pueblo, everything is sacred; theirs is a religion to be lived among the birds and animals and the trees swaying in the light winds. This abiding sense of the divine extends from the soil underfoot to the stars glittering in the night sky. Each creature and every constellation has something to say to the people. The story of their place in nature is told again and again by Pueblo elders, who deeply love the land. The following prayer expresses the viewpoint of the Tewa people.

Tewa Pueblo Prayer

O our mother the earth, O our father the sky,
Your children are we, and with tired backs
We bring you gifts that you love.
Then weave for us a garment of brightness;
May the warp be the white light of morning,
May the weft be the red light of evening,
May the fringes be the falling rain,
May the border be the standing rainbow.
Thus weave for us a garment of brightness
That we may walk fittingly where birds sing
That we may walk fittingly where the grass is green,
O our mother the earth, O our father the sky!

2. At Home in a Dry Land

Beehive ovens dot the yards and plazas of pueblos in New Mexico and Arizona. Women still bake bread in the Spanish-style ovens, as ancestors did for hundreds of years.

MANY CENTURIES BEFORE EUROPEAN EXPLORERS VENTURED INTO THE Western Hemisphere, the Pueblos had created a distinctive, advanced culture in North America. Peace loving, they perfected a city life in harmony with the environment and with each other. Deeply spiritual, they lived their religion on a daily basis and fashioned a just way of governing themselves—along with mastering a magnificent architecture, an impressive system of irrigated agriculture, and a highly refined art of pottery, weaving, jewelry, and leather work.

Adobe Houses

The Anasazi built their early pit house dwellings by digging into the earth to a depth of five to six feet, then building up walls of adobe and wood around the holes to make a circular building. They placed a fire pit for cooking and heating in the center of the pit house beneath a smoke hole in the roof. They used the smoke hole as an entrance, often with the aid of a notched log ladder. Situated below the frost line, with one or two rooms for eating, sleeping, and living, as well as storage, these single-family homes stayed warm during the winter and fairly cool during the heat of summer. However, because the rooms were small and dark with little privacy, people spent most of their life outdoors. Everyone rose with the sun and went to work in an open area called the plaza or in the fields. As the Anasazi began to erect aboveground homes, they kept the pit houses for ceremonies.

Three women and a little girl at Santa Clara Pueblo work together in the plaza outside their adobe homes.

The cliff-dwelling people found building materials all around them—red or yellow sandstone that split easily with stone tools. Hopi, Zuñi, and other Pueblo men laid these thin blocks to form thick walls, filled the cracks with smaller stones, and plastered the surface with mud. Farther east where sandstone was scarce the early Pueblos discovered that they could make homes of the very earth beneath their feet. Much of Arizona and New Mexico is covered with the materials for making adobe, a blend of clay and sand that dries hard as concrete without cracking or shrinking. Some early shelters were made of poles covered with adobe mud. Later, the Pueblos built square pueblos: To make the walls they placed the adobe between two rows of poles. Or they mixed the adobe with small rocks and made the walls one handful at a time. Men journeyed to the mountains and brought back cottonwood logs for the roof beams. Stripping the bark, they laid the logs over the walls, then placed a layer of willow sticks and a bed of grass and brush at right angles to the logs. They plastered the roof with adobe, leaving the ends of the logs sticking out at the tops of the walls. The name for adobe comes from the Spanish language, but was originally from the Arabic words *at-tub* and *tobe*, both of which mean brick. The Spanish were experienced in building with earthen materials, but they used clay bricks. When they arrived in the Southwest, they taught the Pueblos to make adobe bricks for churches, and the Pueblos soon adopted this method instead of laying handfuls of mud for the construction of their homes and ceremonial kivas. They also began to add straw to the adobe mixture to strengthen the bricks.

Beams had to be strong to support both the roof and the floor of multi-storied pueblos. The beams were crisscrossed with small branches and then thickly plastered with adobe.

Whether the buildings were made of split sandstone, poles lined with adobe, or adobe mixed with rocks, the insides of the rooms were coated with a smooth, thin layer of adobe. Sometimes, they were whitewashed with a mixture of gypsum—a powdered mineral—and water. Inside the small, boxlike rooms, the soil floors were hard packed from constant padding of feet. Women swept the houses with brooms made from bunches of grama grass. Sometimes, they made channels or spouts along the edges of the rooms to carry away water from a leak in the roof. In early homes, a hollow in the center of the floor held the fire, its smoke rising through the doorway in the roof. Later, the Pueblos

To enter a home, people had to climb up wooden ladders placed against the wall of the pueblo. Then they descended another ladder through the doorway on the roof, which also served as a smoke hole.

built adobe fireplaces and chimneys in the corners. They lit the fire with torches made from clumps of cedar bark fastened with yucca strings on a stick. A woven yucca grass mat might also adorn the floor. Masonry benches and shelves were often built in; there might be a few wooden blocks for seats as well. Blankets and rabbit skin robes were used for keeping warm. Deer antlers on the wall held clothing; so did a stripped cottonwood pole hung from the rafters with strips of yucca. There would likely be a stewing pot supported by a frame of three adobe knobs sitting over a low fire and other pots and jars for food and water around the room. Gourds were used as dippers, bowls, and bottles.

An opening might be left for the door with a log beam placed across the top. Sometimes, translucent slabs of a stone called selenite were placed in the openings to admit a little sunlight but keep rodents and insects out. Like pit houses, however, most early adobe homes had no windows or doors—they were entered through the roof. Although they made good fortresses, they complicated daily life. Balancing jars of water on their heads, women first climbed up a wooden ladder to the roof of the pueblo, then down into their room on another ladder. Staggering under the weight of a deer or pronghorn carcass, men similarly made the climb up and then down into their safe homes. Women made feather offerings for good luck in ladder climbing and people joked about the shy young man who tumbled down the ladder on a visit to his girlfriend. The Zuñi phrase for entering pueblo rooms is translated as "up the ladder and down the ladder."

When built atop mesas or tucked on canyon ledges, the pueblos offered protection from hostile neighbors and the invading Spanish. Even when the village lay in a valley, people often had a defensive hilltop to which they could retreat if attacked. The buildings were usually clustered, some three or four stories high. Each "apartment complex" housed about two hundred people, with entire families crowded into each single room. With their homes conveniently located near fields of corn, beans, and squash, the inhabitants dried vegetables, stacked firewood, and made pottery outside their doors, often on the roof of the home below, which served as a balcony. Women made wafer bread of blue cornmeal in a special room and baked in pits or later in beehive ovens on the ground below. The dark interior rooms were used for storage of dried foods, firewood, and materials for making pottery and baskets. Sometimes, people stayed in these rooms during the cold winter months; priests stored sacred objects in them or retired there to fast.

Families, Clans, and Villages

The Pueblos have always been guided by their religion, not by politics or material goods, and over time each village developed its own secret rites and traditions. Although today many outwardly follow Christianity, they still devoutly practice their ancient beliefs. The major ceremonies, arranged by the secret societies of the kivas, are held between crop seasons and emphasize prayers and thanksgiving for ample rain and abundant harvests.

*T*his 1852 lithograph by Richard H. Kern depicts a group of Zuñi women grinding corn inside an adobe home. Women who ground corn well were highly regarded in the community.

*W*omen ground corn with a pair of stones. They spread the hard kernels on the larger stone and, gripping the smaller, rubbed back and forth over the corn.

Especially among the western Pueblos, benevolent spirits called kachinas or Cloud Beings are honored as bringers of rain and good will. Their spirits are believed to possess the masked dancers who impersonate them in rituals, and dolls depicting them are given to children. Some of the eastern Pueblos separate their villagers into Summer and Winter People, who alternate responsibility for ceremonies.

Village society has traditionally been organized around the family, often around extended families that include grandparents, aunts, and uncles, as well as larger groups of related people known as clans. Many people were—and still are—members of clans. These clans include the Corn Clan, the Turkey Clan, the Turquoise Clan, and many others. Members may take turns representing the clan in the government of the pueblo and in traditional religious ceremonies.

Early society in most pueblos was matriarchal. Women headed each of the households, which included the mother, grandmother, sisters, and aunts as an extended family. A clan consisted of several households. All the members of a clan were more or less closely related. Among most peoples, descent is matrilineal, that is, traced through the mother's side of the family. Marriage was and still is monogamous, and must be between members of different clans or groups of related clans. Family homes, including all the furnishings, belonged to the wife.

In the village plaza, women came together to grind corn all day on a sandstone slab called a metate. They ground the corn against the metate with another stone called a mano from the Spanish word for "hand." Stones ranging from coarse lava rock to fine sandstone were used to make cornmeal of different textures. Sometimes a man played a wooden flute while the women dragged the stones back and forth over the hard kernels. By age forty most people had worn their teeth down by eating the coarse meal that often included sand from the hand grinding. Nevertheless, corn was the principal crop at the heart of Pueblo life, and it was considered sacred.

Women also made pottery in the plaza. Early in the morning, men began to carve stone buildings or construct adobe dwellings. Others headed to the mountains and brought back timber that they made into beams. Armed with bows and arrows, some men departed early to hunt deer, pronghorns, rabbits, and birds. Men also met with traders, and acquired copper and shells from the coastal waters of California in exchange for pottery and turquoise. The Pueblos also traded for macaws, which they kept not as pets but for the colorful feathers used in religious ceremonies.

Since the days of their Anasazi ancestors, the Pueblo people have kept dogs as pets. The Anasazi kept small dogs with stubby legs that probably resembled modern-day dachshunds. Though not used for hunting, they warned of enemy attack and sometimes accompanied their masters on journeys. They were occasionally eaten, but only when food was scarce. The Pueblos also captured wild turkeys and kept them in coops, not eating them, but using their feathers in ceremonial costumes. They also twisted the feathers into ropes and wove them into warm blankets.

Although the Pueblos worked hard, they enjoyed games, such as throwing dice made of small bones. They also played a game that blended elements of basketball and soccer. In this game, which was played in ancient Mexico and Central America too, contestants tried to knock a hard rubber ball through a hoop using only their feet or head. After the sun had descended over the land, elders told stories. The tales not only entertained young and old, but reminded the Pueblos of their creation. The powerful spoken words could also heal injuries and illness, as well as turn away evil.

3. Lifeways

Today, pottery making has become a highly regarded art form among the Pueblos. The vessel on the left is a wedding vase; the bride and groom each drink from one of the mouths.

AMONG THE PUEBLO, THE COURSE OF LIFE HAS LONG FOLLOWED THE cycles of the earth, sun, and moon. People watched the sun, carefully noting how its position changed slightly with each passing day. They relied upon the location of the sun on the horizon to establish directions, make calendars, plant crops, and hold religious celebrations. They also observed the lengthening days leading to the summer solstice, the longest day of the year, and the shortening days moving toward the winter solstice, or longest night of the year. Everyone pursued both daily tasks and special events—the art of living itself—according to the lessons of the days and the seasons.

Cycle of Life

Birth. The early Pueblos held many magical beliefs about childbirth. A pregnant woman was not to look at anything ugly or scary, otherwise her baby would be marked by misfortune. Similarly, the father was not to hunt or hurt any creature, or the baby might be injured or killed at birth. If the woman unbraided her hair and untied any knots in her clothing, the pain of her delivery would be eased.

Among the Zuñis and Hopis, the mother and sisters looked after the woman during labor, calling in a medicine man only if there were complications, while the eastern Pueblos, especially the Keres, often relied on the medicine man. After delivery, the baby and mother were washed and kept indoors to protect them from danger. The Zuñi lightly covered the baby with ashes, which

Adorned in turquoise-and-silver jewelry, this young woman proudly holds her baby. The peaceful Pueblos tenderly cared for their children, who were much wanted and deeply loved.

they believed held spiritual powers. Among the Zuñi and the Keres, the baby was guarded by a sacred ear of corn.

At dawn the newborn baby was presented to Father Sun. Among the eastern Pueblos, the medicine man named the child. The Hopi and Zuñi, who traced their descent on the mother's side, acknowledged the father's line at this time. During a ceremony, a member of his family carried the baby into the light and chose a name or several names from his clan. The child could later choose a special "sun name."

The baby was swaddled in fur blankets, soft buckskin, or cloth and strapped to a cradleboard with yucca strings or rope. Sometimes cradleboards were made of wicker basketry; others were simply wooden boards that mothers carried on their backs as they worked. The baby remained on the cradleboard day and night for about four months, after which the little one was unstrapped for a while each day. When the child started to walk, it was no longer placed on the cradleboard.

Here is a lovely lullaby that mothers sang to their babies:

There are many sleepy little birds
Sleepy little birds, sleepy little birds.
So go to sleep, my little girl. . . .

Oh come, you sleepy little birds
And slumber on her hollow eyes,
That she may sleep the livelong day,
That she may sleep the livelong night.

Childhood. At the dawn of each new day children were sent outside to sprinkle an offering of sacred corn pollen and say a prayer. Along with the other members of the family, they rolled up blankets and fur robes and hung them on a pole.

Children had a breakfast of corn mush sometimes enriched with a few seeds. Younger children stayed close to their mothers as they swept the earthen floor and set about their work for the day—grinding corn, weaving at the loom, or making pottery. The

From their fathers, boys learned to cultivate corn and other crops. They also mastered the art of weaving and making handicrafts. This boy is practicing to be a hunter with a small bow and arrow.

older boys, however, stripped off their clothing and bathed in a nearby stream or spring. They believed they would be strengthened by the chill water. Then they joined the men in the fields where they helped to plant, cultivate, irrigate, and harvest crops of corn, beans, and squash.

Children learned by watching their parents and other adults in the village. Boys learned to raise crops and hunt game, as well as weave at the loom. Girls became skilled at preparing food and taking care of the home. Among the western Pueblos, the mother's brother often guided the children, who were rarely scolded. They were simply told what was right. Children were not whipped—there is an old story about a child who ran away after a beating and never returned to the village. Sometimes, a "bogeyman" wearing a scary mask visited the village and confronted a child who misbehaved. The parents promised that their child would do better; otherwise the wild-haired creature would return to the village. Other times, the gentle kachinas came to the village, bringing rain, blessings upon the people, and small gifts, especially for the children. A boy might pray for a bow and arrow while a little girl might long for a kachina doll.

Coming-of-Age. At puberty, boys and girls were initiated into the mysteries of Pueblo life, especially religious secrets and marriage. Pictographs, or drawings, of these ceremonies decorate the walls of many kivas. The young people were never to reveal these secrets—the powers would be lost if strangers knew of them. In

With their hair elaborately styled, these Hopi girls have come of age. They are ready to marry and have their own homes, where they will raise their own children just as their mothers once cared for them.

later years, when the Spanish tried to destroy their religion, the Pueblo guarded their beliefs even more carefully.

When she came of age, at about twelve, a Hopi girl ground corn for four days behind a curtain away from the sun, just as women hid themselves from the sun at childbirth. Afterwards, she had her hair done up in a butterfly style that indicated she was ready for marriage.

A boy might meet a girl as she fetched water at a nearby spring, or they might catch each other's eye at a ceremony. The rabbit hunt, however, was a special matchmaking occasion among the Pueblos. When a boy killed a rabbit the girls ran to him, and he presented it to the first girl to reach him. That evening, or the next day, she offered him some cooked food in return, possibly leading to courtship and marriage.

Among the western Pueblos, the girls frequently pursued the boys, presenting them with gifts of food. A girl might tell the young man's mother, "I have come to marry your son." Among the eastern Pueblos, the boys typically initiated courtship, although he might be rejected, or "given the squash." In all Pueblo groups, the parents had to consent to the marriage.

Marriage. The Hopis held elaborate courtship rituals in which the bride presented corn cakes to the groom. When he accepted, she went to his house to grind corn for four days to impress him with her skill. Meanwhile, the men in the family wove her wedding trousseau from cotton. Today, the eastern Pueblos are often married by Catholic priests. However, the two-mouthed wedding jar is still used. The bride and the groom both drink from this jar as a symbol of their unity.

Whatever the manner of their marriage, the couple settled down with older members of the family. After the exchange of gifts, the Hopi bride took her husband to live in her mother's home, as did the Zuñi. Among the eastern Pueblos, the couple lived with the groom's family or the husband built a separate home for his young bride and himself. When they had children, aunts and uncles helped to raise them. If one or both of the parents died or if the couple divorced, these relatives continued to look after the children. Divorce has always been fairly common, the Pueblo believing that a couple that doesn't get along shouldn't stay together. Traditionally, a man living with his wife's family simply gathered his clothes and returned to his mother. A woman living with her husband's family went back to her mother. In either case, the children stayed in the home where they were born.

Death. With old age came wisdom, and the elderly were very much honored among the Pueblos. When too old to work in the fields, a man taught others. He might hold a position on the village council or help look after his grandchildren while their father was in the fields. An old woman showed her granddaughters how to grind corn and cook over a fire. Among the western Pueblos, she held important property and kept a shrine in her home.

The Pueblos often prayed to enjoy a long life. When they passed away, preferably at an old age, it was believed that they traveled four days to the Land of the Dead. Relatives carefully washed the body, dressed the deceased in their finest clothing, and painted the face. This was all done quickly because the Pueblos worried that the departed longed to take someone with them. If they stayed with the body too long, they too might be snatched away. Early Pueblos carefully laid the body in a sitting position in burial pits lined with bark or grass. Believing in an afterlife, they placed new, unworn sandals with the deceased, along with food, baskets, nets, jewelry, stone pipes, digging sticks, and weapons. They next covered the body with more bark or grass, then slabs of stone, wooden poles, brush, and soil. In the dry climate, the bodies have been naturally preserved for hun-

The elders of the pueblo instructed others in arts and crafts and in the skills needed for survival. Here, young and old pause from their work and pose together in the village plaza.

dreds of years. Because they were too young to find their way to the other world, children were buried under the floor so their spirits could enter any new babies born in the home.

It was believed that the departed lingered around the village for four days, and each day family members brought food and water to the grave. On the fourth day, family members purified themselves by washing their hair, clothes, and perhaps the house itself—or they fumigated the home with smoke. They removed all traces of the dead so that the underworld would no longer have a hold on the living. Even dreaming of the dead was believed to make one ill, so with the exception of those who had lost a mate, they concentrated on their work. Widows and widowers were required to mourn and make special offerings for six months or a year, after which they could marry again.

In the Land of the Dead, the deceased lived as they had on Earth, except that everything was in reverse—winter was summer and night was day. In some cases the dead might become Cloud Beings with the power to send rain.

Hunting and Gathering

The early Pueblos gathered wild foods and hunted deer, pronghorns, and mountain sheep, along with badgers, foxes, wolves, and cougars. They needed furs and skins for clothing and drums, and sinew for bowstrings, sewing thread, and fasteners for tools. They shaped bones into tools and made hooves into rattles.

In more recent times, the people who lived near the Great Plains made long journeys in pursuit of buffalo herds. Near home, they hunted gophers, ground squirrels, and especially rabbits. Men relied upon smooth, heavy rabbit clubs to skillfully bring down these fleet-footed creatures. Resembling boomerangs, the curved weapons were thrown at the quarry, thus saving arrows for other prey. The Hopis preferred a unique rabbit club that bounced on the ground. With each throw, they might strike several rabbits fleeing through the brush.

Occasionally, a man hunted alone, patiently stalking a deer all day and night. When the deer became hungry and tired, he could catch it and wrestle it down by hand. Other times, men journeyed forth in small hunting parties. Working together, men, women, and children sometimes joined in the hunt. They drove the game into a canyon or corral, then quickly killed the rabbits, deer, and other animals with clubs. Or they stampeded herds of pronghorn and deer past waiting hunters or over the rim of a canyon. Or the group formed a circle in an area that they gradually tightened in a "surround hunt." Community hunts, as well as corn shucking, were opportunities for much socializing and occasional courtship. All Pueblos also had ceremonial rabbit hunts when meat was needed for a feast; only the men went on these hunts.

Often, men trapped rabbits, prairie dogs, and other small animals, as well as coyotes, with simple, yet ingenious deadfalls. One end of a heavy log or a large flat stone was propped up with a stick to which a small amount of bait was attached. When the rabbit or

*B*efore a hunt, people often gathered and prayed that they might find abundant game. This watercolor by Gilbert Atencio entitled Blessing of the Deer Dance *depicts one of these important ceremonies.*

T he Pueblos have long honored the eagle, whose feathers adorned their ceremonial dress. In Eagle Dancer, *Raymond Naha has painted two young men in feathered garb dancing to the accompaniment of a drum.*

gopher tugged at the bait, the stick was pulled loose and the heavy log or stone abruptly dropped, killing the luckless creature.

A man could never have too many feathers, and small birds were often caught with nooses made of human hair. Tied to sticks, the nooses were spread along the ground with a scattering of seeds, and "the birds of summer," also referred to as "the rain bringers," caught their feet in the nearly invisible threads. To catch an eagle, whose feathers were especially prized, a man built a little stone shelter or dug a pit with sticks laid across the top. Placing a dead rabbit on top, he hid inside until an eagle swooped down.

He then snatched the great bird by the legs and shoved its head into the sand to smother it. Only the Isleta shot eagles with arrows—most Pueblos believed they must not spill the blood of this proud bird. All hunters made an offering when they killed an eagle.

Climbing high up in the cliffs, Hopi men also raided eagle nests "owned" by a particular clan. They brought back the young birds in cradleboards and tied them to the roofs of their houses. Fed meat and named like their own children, the eaglets were raised for their feathers. When grown, they were killed in a special ritual and their feathers were used to adorn prayer sticks and the costumes of the dancers. The bodies of the dead birds were buried in special eagle cemeteries.

Sacred Corn and Other Crops

The Pueblos raised beans and squash, but corn was by far the most important crop. This grain was so vital to their survival that the Zuñi honored the Corn Maidens, whose flesh was corn, and the Keres believed in the Corn Mother, who provided this magical food. Virtually all ceremonies involved this grain, and corn pollen was often scattered when one asked a favor of the supernatural.

The Pueblos grew several different types of corn, including hard-kerneled flint corn that stores well for many years and flour corn that grinds readily. The Pueblos probably did not have sweet corn and popcorn until European traders and trappers brought it to them from other Indian tribes. Over the years, however, they developed many different varieties of corn in bright colors—blue, black (actually deep purple), reddish, and speckled, as well as white and yellow. The four most common colors represented the four directions: north (yellow), south (red), west (blue), and east (white). Praying as they planted, men kept the seeds carefully separated, but cross-pollination as the corn grew resulted in ears of multiple colors.

The Pueblos who had moved to the Rio Grande were reasonably safe from drought, but others worried over possible catastrophe through the long growing season. Many villages depended on rainfall as well as the water from nearby streams. The Hopi were fortunate if one or two showers darkened the soil between the May planting and the August harvest. The people used a planting stick to dig a hole, as deep as eighteen inches, so the corn seeds would be closer to moisture well beneath the surface of the ground. They placed their fields on fan-shaped slopes that caught any runoff and built small dams across creek beds to hold rainwater. They also shaped ridges of soil around each plant to catch the water until their fields looked like waffles. All Pueblos held many rituals to encourage rainfall, for example, racing through the fields to draw storm fronts over them and praying that irrigation ditches would be filled with water.

According to Zuñi belief, a comfortable life on Earth is made possible by the four elements and corn. This is expressed in a stanza from one of their songs:

*I*n Pueblo Family Group *by Cochití artist Justino Herrera, the parents and the son each sprinkle corn pollen as they walk along the path of life.*

The sun, who is Father of all,
The earth, who is the Mother of men,
The water, who is the Grandfather,
The fire, who is the Grandmother,
Our brothers and sisters the Corn
and seeds of growing things.

The Pueblos dropped as many as twenty seeds in each hole in the hope that at least a few might survive the harsh climate. The plants grew in short, tough clumps that withstood the driving winds and dry soil. People formed hoeing parties to keep weeds away from the plants, but they were careful not to scrape too deep into the hard surface lest moisture escape. The Zuñi, in particular, went to elaborate lengths to keep hungry birds away, especially crows. They stretched a network of strings on sticks hung with sticky cactus leaves and layed out hair nooses to snare crows, and they fashioned hideous scarecrows to frighten them off. As the corn ripened, children and old people watched over the fields, shouting and throwing rocks at the hungry birds.

The Zuñis and Hopis roasted milky young ears of corn in large pits ten to twelve feet deep and three feet wide. Kindling was first placed in the pits and allowed to burn down to ashes. The unhusked ears were then placed in the pit, and hot coals were piled over them. Slowly roasting from late afternoon to daybreak, the corn was the first fresh food of the season. People also enjoyed corn cakes made from juicy kernels scraped from the cob.

When the corn matured to hard kernels of many colors every pueblo held celebrations. The whole village was swept clean before the first ears of corn were carried reverently into each home, sprinkled with cornmeal, and placed in the storeroom. Families came together to husk the piles of corn, boys and girls taking advantage of the gathering to flirt with one another. The best ears were put aside for next year's seed, the husks and stems braided, and the bunches of brightly colored corn hung on the walls. The rest of the corn was either spread out on the roof or hung from the doorways. The women continued to dry the corn, tossing out moldy ears and grinding the kernels into meal.

The Pueblos also raised two kinds of squash, a large green variety and a small striped one. People relied upon two types of beans as well—a large kidney bean grown by Indians throughout the Americas and one called a tepary, which is known only in Mexico and the Southwest. Growing wild in northern Mexico and the canyons of Arizona, the red, white, and spotted tepary beans have been found in Anasazi ruins. Beans were an excellent source of protein for the Pueblos, who did not eat much meat. The Hopis planted a small variety of sunflower that now grows wild along western roadways. They used the seeds as a source of oil and ate them roasted as well.

When the Spanish arrived, the Pueblos began to raise wheat, threshing the grain on circles of hard-packed ground. They also began to grow peppers—both chili and bell—as well as tomatoes, peas, onions, watermelons, and other fruits and vegetables. They planted orchards of peaches and apricots, which were split in half and dried in the sun.

Preparing Food

Along with grinding corn and making pottery, women undertook the challenging task of feeding their families. They gathered seeds, berries, and nuts. Piñon nuts were an especially valued source of wild foods, though corn likely made up three-fourths of their diet. To prepare corn for cooking, Pueblo girls and women spent three to four hours each day grinding the hard kernels between flat stones, sometimes to the accompaniment of music. If the corn became moist, they might toast the cracked kernels in a pot over the fire. A woman was able to produce three to four quarts of cornmeal a day.

Cornmeal was used in dumplings, gruel, and especially bread. A thin wafer bread, called piki (pee-kee) from the Hopi word, was the most popular among the Pueblos. To make it, a flat stone was raised on four other stones so a fire could be built underneath. When this stone griddle became hot the women greased the smooth surface and spread cornmeal batter over it with their fingers. The thin layer cooked almost instantly and was peeled away, then piled in a dish. Some Pueblos, especially the Hopi and the Zuñi, still make wafer bread, using blue cornmeal.

Sometimes, women made a thicker bread, mixing slaked lime and water into the cornmeal to give it a greenish cast. Or they cooked up cornmeal dumplings. Or they placed meat in dough, which was then wrapped in a cornhusk and boiled to make a favorite dish known by its Mexican Indian name as tamale. To make gruel, the Pueblos poured cornmeal into boiling water. Sometimes, like Indians in the East, they made hominy by soaking the kernels until the shells broke off. Women then ground up the swollen kernels and made thin pancakes called tortillas. Before they had coffee, they enjoyed a cornmeal drink as a morn-

*L*oaves of bread are baked in ovens located outside, often in the backyard. The horno, as the oven is called, is made of adobe.

*T*o heat the oven, women start a fire inside. Once the fire has burned down, they scrape out the ashes. Then, kneeling in front, they slide loaves in and out with a wooden paddle.

ing beverage, a special traveling drink. The Pueblos also used corn as a sweetener.

After the Spanish arrived, women began to bake wheat bread in a beehive oven called a *horno*. Sometimes, they sprouted wheat, which they then ground up and mixed with dough to make a sweet bread. Still used today, the dome-shaped ovens have a single door, just large enough so that a flat wooden paddle may be slid inside to place and remove the loaves of bread. At the top there is a hand-sized vent.

First, a woman makes a fire inside the baking chamber. When the fire has burned down, having thoroughly heated the oven, the woman sweeps out the ashes and slides the small round loaf inside. Almost every Pueblo family had one of these ovens near their home, and many still do.

Fresh squash was roasted, or strips of it were dried for the lean winter. Strips were made by peeling squash, cutting it into spirals, drying it, and rolling it into little bundles for storage. These strips were later soaked in water to bring back their flavor and included in a variety of delicious dishes. Squash seeds were ground to release cooking oil. Beans were boiled, and sometimes leftovers were pounded into a paste and mixed with cornmeal to make wafer bread. Beans and other vegetables were also cooked in stews with meat and corn.

The Pueblos included many roots, greens, berries, seeds, and nuts from wild plants in their diet. Wild onions and potatoes, along with the roots of the blazing star plant and the leaves of the

Pueblo Hamburger Stew

This modern version of a traditional dish, which once included wild game and later lamb and mutton, has long been a favorite among the Pueblos. It can easily be made today.

Ingredients:

2 pounds lean ground beef
1 large onion, chopped
5 medium potatoes, peeled
   and sliced thin
2 tablespoons cooking oil

Pour oil in frying pan. Add onion and cook until softened. Add hamburger and slowly brown. Drain off excess fat.

Add potatoes along with just enough water to prevent sticking to the pan. Cover and simmer until potatoes are soft (about 1/2 hour). If desired, add salt to taste.

This dish may be varied by adding chopped green chilies, tomatoes, corn kernels, or green peas.

Rocky Mountain bee plant, were also important sources of nutrition. The leaves and stalks of the Rocky Mountain bee were boiled down to make a black syrup used for decorating pottery. The hardened cakes could also be broken up and cooked as food during the winter when fresh vegetables were scarce. Juniper berries, nuts from the piñon tree, the fruit of yucca plants, and prickly pear cactus were often eaten while people waited for the corn to ripen. The Pueblos also made chewing gum from milkweed, chicory, and cattails and harvested or traded for tobacco, which adults smoked rolled in cornhusks or in clay or stone pipes. Young men were not allowed to smoke until they had proven themselves as hunters or warriors. Even then, they were not allowed to smoke in the presence of their elders until they were married.

Meat was roasted over fires in hunting camps. Back in the villages, women boiled meat along with corn and vegetables, in stews. They also sliced venison and buffalo meat into strips, which were cured in the hot sun to make jerky. The term *jerky* comes from a Peruvian word translated into Spanish as *charqui* (charkee), or sun-dried meat. The stiff hard strips were soaked in water and boiled. Salt was highly valued by the Pueblos, most of whom traveled to a lake south of Zuñi country to collect the sacred mineral. The Hopis had their own salt spring in the canyon of the Little Colorado River.

Some of the interesting dishes prepared by the Pueblos to this very day are Pueblo oven bread, Zuñi steamed bread, blue corn bread, blue corn mush, green pumpkin stew, green chili stew, red chili stew, Pueblo calabacitas, Hopi scalloped red peppers and corn, Pueblo chili fritters, meat jerky, Pueblo dried red chili fry, Pueblo green jerky fry, dried corn with lamb, Zuñi sunflower gravy, and wheat pudding dessert.

Both dried red chilies and green chilies have been important hot and spicy seasonings since they were acquired from the Spanish. Green chilies are roasted by laying them out on a cookie sheet or aluminum foil on an oven rack, which is placed in the lower broiler position. The chilies are broiled until blisters form on the skin. They are then turned and broiled on the other side. Roasted green chilies may be used immediately or placed in plastic bags and frozen for later use.

Clothing and Jewelry

In the days of the Anasazi, people wore skirts and breechcloths made of animal skins, willow bark, or yucca leaves. They either went barefoot or wore sandals of woven yucca strips and hemp. Later, they adopted moccasins and leggings from the Apaches or Plains tribes who lived to the north of their villages. During the hot summer months, people dressed lightly. In the winter they wrapped themselves in leather cloaks and fur blankets. Large animals, such as bears, were scarce in the desert country so they stitched rabbit skins together to make robes. They also raised turkeys and wove the feathers with yucca twine into wraps that kept them warm in the winter.

Along with the Pima and Papago, the Pueblos were one of the few native peoples of North America to wear cotton garments instead of animal skins. By A.D. 800 they had learned about cotton from their southern neighbors in Mexico and had begun to grow their own. The fibers were spun into thread, then woven into

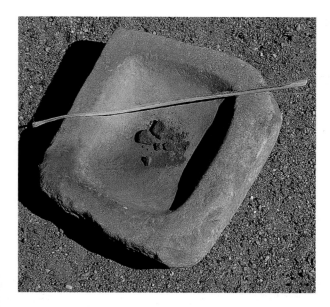

Dyes were used both to adorn pottery and to color garments. Most were made from natural materials—dried plants or ground-up minerals. The reddish brown color shown here was very popular.

cloth. The cotton fabric was dyed with natural pigments obtained from plants and minerals. Deep yellow, reddish brown, and a luminous blue-green were favorite colors.

Men typically wore a strip of white cotton cloth, called a breechcloth, between their legs, while for ceremonies they wound a white cotton kilt around their waist. The edges of these garments were often embroidered with geometric designs in shades of blue along with hints of red, brown, and green. A cotton or wool sash brocaded with green and brown was added for ceremonies. They also wore braided sashes with heavy cotton knobs woven over cornhusks where the fringe joins the cloth. Sometimes they wore a sort of poncho—a piece of cloth with a hole for the head—that draped over their shoulders, back, and chest. Later, they made embroidered cotton shirts with sleeves similar to those worn by the Spanish. Over time, men also began to wear woolen blankets, as well as buckskin moccasins and leggings, instead of fur and feather robes.

Women have long worn dresses or shawls called mantas, made of leather or creamy white cotton that is either plainly

Here, a group of Zuñi men pose in clothing that blends traditional and Spanish elements—headbands and considerable jewelry, as well as cloth garments and leather boots.

Among the Pueblos, men have traditionally been the weavers. Here, a Hopi man carefully inspects a hand-woven ceremonial belt, or sash, with long knotted braids at each end.

woven or has a zigzag design stitched diagonally into the garment. The dresses were traditionally dark blue, although Zuñi and Hopi dresses were usually black or sometimes brown. Shawls might be embroidered or bordered in red. Women wore belts of yucca or cedar fiber and later cotton. Today, belts are made of wool. About three to five inches wide, they are long enough to wrap twice around the waist. They are usually red or green with strands of white woven into the cloth in geometric designs. In the past, women wore moccasins, like men, although they were shaped like a boot and rubbed to a gleaming white with clay. Reaching almost to the knee, they were so valuable they were worn only for ceremonies.

All the villagers adorned themselves with rings, bracelets, necklaces, and pendants. Men wore as much jewelry as women—strings of turquoise and necklaces of black jet, white shells, and red shells. Men braided their hair while women chose from a variety of fancy styles. Men usually wore their hair long, sometimes tied in a double knot for ceremonies. They either parted their hair down the middle and bound it into two braids with brightly colored yarn or they clipped neat bangs in what some people call a terrace haircut. Women often wore their hair in a terrace style tied with string in the back.

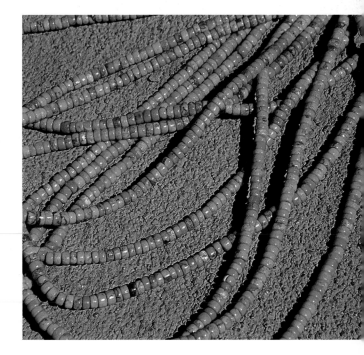

Among the Pueblos, turquoise has long been a popular stone used in making necklaces, bracelets, and rings. Seeds and glass beads are also common.

When they came of age, however, Hopi women wound their hair over cornhusks to form round flat disks on either side or over bent willow frames to resemble butterfly wings. After they married, women wore their hair in two braids.

In the past, both men and women frequently washed their hair with a sudsy shampoo made from the yucca plant. With grama grass or purple-hair grass brushes, they combed out their long hair, often as part of village ceremonies. Usually individuals groomed themselves, but husbands and wives combed each other's hair as an expression of love, and young couples did so to indicate their engagement.

Both men and women relied on cosmetics and perfumes from wild herbs and animal tallow, or fat. In preparation for ceremonies, men smeared tallow on their faces and bodies, then made designs with black soot, crushed yellow sunflower petals, or red, yellow, and white powder from various clays. Women dabbed red spots on their faces with crushed amaranth blossoms. They also placed sumac buds in their clothes as perfume or chewed thistle blossoms and rubbed them over their skin. To avoid sunburn both men and women sometimes smeared themselves with crushed mustard leaves.

The Pueblos traded with the Spanish for wool, which they wove into blankets that replaced the rabbit skin robes. They began to make heavy wool dresses, which kept the women warm in the chill days and nights of winter. They also acquired dyes from the Spanish. They especially like the reds, which were not possible to make with vegetable dyes, and they traded for bayenta cloth. Unraveling this red cloth, they wove it as borders or stripes into their own fine garments. They favored the dark blue color obtained from indigo as well. In the past, the Pueblos may have gotten some indigo from the Mexican Indians, but the Spanish brought large amounts of the plant into the region. The color became so popular that some people made all their dresses of a dark blue. Many still do.

Navajo women are remarkable weavers, but among the Pueblos, it is the men who do the weaving. Along with knitting and sewing techniques, the Pueblos learned about looms from the Spanish. Previously, they had stitched fabric or skins together by punching holes in the edges with a bone awl, then pulling string through them. But they soon mastered the art of European dressmaking and tailoring. With the arrival of the Americans and the railroad came calico and silk and later factory-made cloth. Today, most Pueblos wear modern clothes, except during their frequent ceremonies. Along with their everyday clothes, they may also wear a headband or kerchief and moccasins. Women may also choose to put on their old blanket dresses or to wrap themselves in a warm shawl or manta.

Pottery Making

To this day, Pueblo women make lovely pottery. They first grind the clay to remove any lumps. They next moisten and temper, or strengthen, the clay with sand, crushed rocks, or ground

Since the time of the Anasazi, the Pueblos have been skilled potters. Instead of relying on a potter's wheel, they carefully shaped the clay by hand. Here, a woman shows how the clay is coiled to make a pot.

pottery fragments, to prevent the vessel from breaking when fired. Instead of using a potter's wheel, they lay coils to make walls that are then shaped by hand. They decorate the pots, allow them to dry, then fire them by covering them with dried dung, which is then set ablaze. Originally, most of the pots were made with round bottoms, because they were set on soft dirt, not on flat tables or shelves.

The Anasazi probably learned about clayware from Mexican and Central American traders and they quickly became accomplished potters. They first made gray, unpolished vessels, but then began to color their pots with paints made from plant and mineral dyes. Soon they were making jars, bowls, mugs, dippers, and pitchers, as well as round pots. Among the best-known pottery is the black-on-white style of the Kayenta region. This was replaced by a yellow-on-black style and the Hopi pottery of many colors. Pottery making reached its height between A.D. 1100 and 1300, but the strong tradition is still carried on—and enhanced—by skilled Pueblo women whose work has risen to an art form. Seldom repeating the same design, they decorate the clay vessels with highly original swirls and zigzags. They have long been admired for their imaginative designs, and even today women "dream their pottery."

Travel and Trade

Since their environment provided for most of their needs, the Pueblos did not wander like the Apaches, Navajos, and other nomadic peoples. Yet they liked to trade their pottery, woven blankets, and jewelry, journeying to other pueblos when they heard people needed their goods. On clear days, they gathered in the village plaza, spread out their handiwork, and bartered with whomever might be interested.

The Apaches also came to Pueblo villages with coiled baskets, as well as buckskin and moccasins, which they traded for cornmeal, squash, turquoise, and cotton clothing. The Navajos brought horses and sheep taken from the Spanish in night raids, as well as firewood and animal skins. The Paiute also swapped horses, along with sturdy bows for bringing down deer and pronghorns. The Yuma and Mohave traded parrot feathers and shells from the Pacific Ocean, both of which were highly desired by the Pueblos, as well as face paints acquired from other tribes.

Most often these traders came to the Pueblos. Yet when the Pueblos went on occasional buffalo hunts, they bartered for dried meat, buffalo hides, and leather goods with the tribes of the Great Plains. Trade with other villages and distant tribes, from the Gulf of California to the prairies of the heartland, went on for over a thousand years. When the Spanish and then the Americans came to the Southwest, the Pueblos traded with them. A lively exchange is still carried on in the plaza at Santa Fe and in many villages of New Mexico.

Playing Games

During peaceful times, people labored around their homes or in the fields. Yet, when they were caught up on their work, they loved to play games, often for days at a time. Everyone, not just the children, took part in these events, which were believed to be ordained by the gods. In fact, the Pueblos still believe that the gods originally played these games not simply for amusement, but to keep the sun arcing across the sky each day, to bring a veil of rain, and to predict the future. In the view of the Pueblos, the

Races were more than entertainment—they had profound religious significance. This 1959 oil painting by Dorothy Brett depicts the sun races held at the Taos Pueblo in northern New Mexico.

balls, darts, and dice of the games were as pleasing to the gods as offerings of cornmeal and turquoise.

People held footraces, usually in the spring and early summer. The Hopi believed the races helped the streams to flow down to the valleys, and the Tewa believed they kept the sun on its proper course. In the kick race, which was popular with the western Pueblos, barefoot runners kicked a stick or ball over a long-distance course of twenty to forty miles through the desert. Supposedly invented by the two gods of war, the race was originally run by two impish children who could change themselves into great heroes. Stories were often told of runaway children who encountered them in the back country and played with them.

Among the Tewa, the most popular spring game was called shinny. Played with a curved branch and deerskin ball filled with a wad of deer hair, this game amounted to a race in which men ran across the fields knocking the ball with their shinny sticks. Sometimes, for ceremonial purposes, the ball was filled with seeds. If the ball split open, scattering the seeds, the Pueblo believed they would have good crops that year. The Tiwa, who live east and south of the Tewa, held relay races along a straight track, running back and forth until one team was an entire "lap" ahead of the other. During this race, which was supposed to ensure that the water flowed in the streams, contestants wore feathers to help them sprint lightly as birds over the land.

The Pueblos played many other games with sticks and stones just for fun. They enjoyed a game similar to horseshoes in which they threw rocks to knock down a stone or corncob that had been stood upright some distance away. In a similar game, women placed necklaces on the stones—the winner was the one who knocked the necklace off the stone. Practicing to be hunters, boys threw rabbit sticks at mountain goat horns scattered over the ground. If a boy struck one, he could claim the horn and continue to "hunt" until he missed, much like boys play marbles today.

Tiwa men used bows and arrows to shoot at small disks of cornhusks about eight inches in diameter. The first arrow to strike the disk became the "bull's eye." The first person to strike that arrow claimed it; the team to win all the arrows of the other team won the contest. Zuñi boys placed a bundle of cornhusks on the ground, often burying the bundle, so contestants had to guess when they shot their arrows at a bump in the earth.

During the winter, the Pueblos played darts, another game from the gods. Using a ball of yucca string for a target, they threw darts made of corncobs with a thin, pointed stick protruding from the end. The missiles were tufted with hawk feathers to guide their flight. The contestant who hit the ball most often won the game. Sometimes, they used reeds as targets and tried to hit each other's darts, claiming those darts whose feathers were touched by another dart. The Pueblos played these games not only to bring rain but to entertain themselves, and they eagerly betted on the outcome.

They also loved stories, many of which involved races. Here's one similar to the classic contest between the tortoise and the hare:

"Coyote and Cottontail: A Tale About Tails"

One time Too-wháy-deh, the Coyote, came to visit Pee-oo-ée-deh, the Cottontail, who sat at the door of his home in the brush.

"What are you thinking?" asked Coyote.

"I am wondering why some animals have large tails and others have short tails," Cottontail said with a sorrowful face. "If we rabbits had long tails like you, we could run fast and true, but now we can only hop."

"Friend, you may be quicker than you think. Let us race around the world," suggested Coyote, who believed he could trick the little rabbit. "Whoever comes in first will kill and eat the other."

"Very well," said the Cottontail meekly. "We may have the race in four days."

Licking his chops, Coyote went home very happy, because he was certain that he would win the race. However, Cottontail had an idea. He went to visit the other rabbits of his tribe and told them of his plan.

On the day of the race, Coyote boasted, "I will win. Why not let me eat you now before you are tired?"

Rabbit answered, "The end of the race is far away. We can run to each of the four corners of the world—east, north, west, and south. Only I will race under the ground, which is easier for me."

Coyote agreed because he was confident he would win.

At the start, the captain shouted, "Haí-koo!"

Coyote sprinted forth, his legs churning furiously. Cottontail scurried into a hole and threw dirt with his hind feet as he dug.

For many days Coyote ran eastward, the Cottontail nowhere in sight. As he turned north, however, Cottontail—or so Coyote thought—sprang from the ground, raced ahead of him, and shot into another hole where he dug once again. Actually, it was not Cottontail, but one of the other rabbits from his tribe.

"Ah, I wish I could run under the ground," sighed Coyote. "It seems so easy for Cottontail."

Coyote ran harder; he came to the north—the end of the world. When he turned west, there was Cottontail once again—or so Coyote thought. The little rabbit taunted him, then plunged into another hole just ahead of him. With a heavy heart, Coyote raced westward. "How can Cottontail run so fast?" he asked himself. Exhausted, his tongue hanging out of his mouth, Coyote turned southward, but a rabbit again appeared just ahead of him. Coyote sprinted toward the finish line where they had begun the race, but there was Cottontail, having already completed the circle.

Calmly grooming himself, Cottontail asked, "Why do we do this to each other?"

Coyote had no answer.

"I have been waiting for you a long time," said Cottontail. "I guess long tails do not help animals run fast. Now come here so that I may eat you, although I am sure that you are tough and stringy."

However, being a coward, Coyote ran away. Later, he learned how Cottontail had tricked him. Since that day, he has eagerly pursued Cottontail, doing his best to get even, by gobbling up as many of the little rabbits as possible.

4. Beliefs

Living in harmony with the earth, people pray for a bountiful harvest or a good hunt, as well as for adequate rain during the growing season. They often hold ceremonies in which drummers beat a rhythm for costumed dancers.

LIKE OTHER NATIVE PEOPLES OF THE AMERICAS, THE PUEBLOS BELIEVED that the divine is present in nature—in stones and stars as well as in people, animals, and plants. Hunters sent forth prayers asking to find game among the trees and grasses. When an animal was about to be killed or a plant harvested, forgiveness was asked for taking its life. To the Pueblos, religion, nature, and art are all blended into everyday life. The Pueblos live on the earth and are sustained by the soil. They dance their prayers upon the earth and they ask for the sun or rain needed to grow their corn. Many rituals have to do with corn, which is the source of life in their culture. They have always devoted much thought and energy to the soil and the rain. By thinking about their corn, the Hopi believed they could make it grow better. Through dances and prayers they believed they could influence the universe by encouraging rain to fall from the sky.

Kivas

When the Pueblos began to construct homes aboveground they used their old pit houses as meeting places for men and as rooms for special ceremonies. Archaeologists who studied the Anasazi called them kivas. Many of the circular rooms had a sipapu, or hole of emergence, in the center of the floor that joined the people with the spirits underground. People used a wooden ladder to climb down into the kiva. Drawings called pictographs and carvings called petroglyphs were made on the interior walls of chambers. They depict mythical figures, as well as geometric

*P*eople climb up these stairs, then descend a slender wooden ladder to enter the underground chamber of this kiva in San Ildefonso Pueblo north of Santa Fe, New Mexico.

designs and everyday activities, such as hunting. Later, the Pueblos hid from Spanish and American invaders in the kivas. To this day, outsiders are not allowed to enter these holy places.

Healings took place in the sacred chambers as well as religious rituals. Drummers pounded out a steady, rhythmic beat as dancers drew forth the divine forces from deep within the earth. Men also wove cotton and told stories in the kivas. Sometimes, as in ancient times, ceremonies are held on the roofs of the kivas, which are usually located in the village plaza.

*G*roups of dancers in ceremonial dress usually advance in a processional style, as shown in this mural painted by a Pueblo artist at the Pueblo Cultural Center in Albuquerque.

Among the hundreds of kivas in little villages scattered throughout the Southwest there were also Great Kivas where large numbers of people came together. Eight have been found at Chaco Canyon along with several others in the region. The kiva at Pueblo Bonito resembles a coliseum. It is believed that people traveled, often long distances, to the Great Kivas. Today, most villages have smaller kivas. Most Pueblos still visit the kiva in their village and take part in seasonal dances and they continue to live their ancient religion not only in dances and ceremonial occasions but over the course of each and every day. Theirs is a religion of the earth, and they respect all of creation, from the soil under their feet to the stars high up in the sky.

Ceremonies and Dances

The Spanish established missions in each of the pueblos and forced the Pueblos to convert to Christianity. Outwardly, people embraced the "new religion," but secretly they continued to practice their own beliefs and rituals, their chants and dances. Dressed

Most often ceremonies within the kiva are held in private. Only people in the pueblo may descend into the holy chamber and take part. Here, we have a rare glimpse of a drummer inside the kiva.

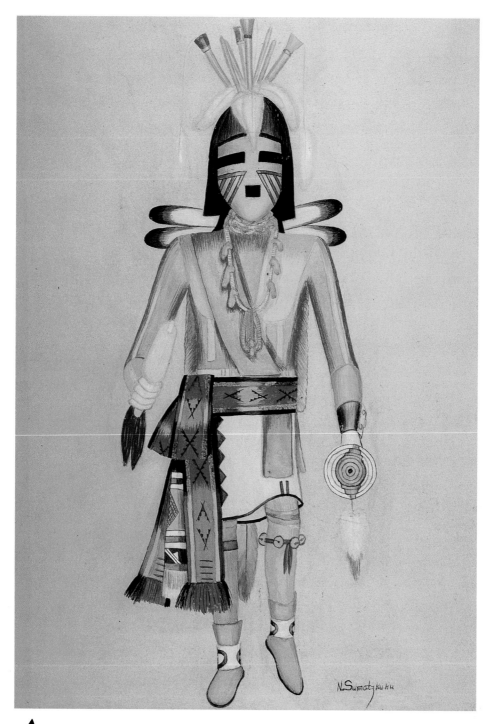

Among the Pueblos, the kachinas, or Spirit Beings, are represented by masked dancers in ceremonial dress. This 1950 watercolor by N. Sumatzkuku, a Hopi artist, depicts a kachina dancer.

in elaborate costumes, often with masks, they held many celebrations throughout the year. Those in honor of the kachinas were the most important.

Kachinas are Spirit Beings, but they may be represented by masked dancers or by dolls made for children to help them learn about Pueblo beliefs. There have been at least 250 different kachinas named, each with its own story. Friendly spirits, they were believed to bring rain and adundant crops. Every village had at least one Kachina Society through which they honored and sought favors of the spirit beings, and the Kachina Dances were the most important rituals of the village. The Pueblos held numerous other dances throughout the years. There were animal dances in which participants dressed as buffalo, deer, pronghorns, and especially the eagle. There was also the Hopi Snake Dance. The corn, rain, and harvest dances are among the many seasonal celebrations.

The Pueblos continue to practice their ancient beliefs deep within the kivas and outside in the village plaza. Many of the dances of the eastern Pueblos are open to the public, and visitors are allowed to respectfully watch the procession of costumed men. Blending ancient beliefs with Christianity, many dances are now held during holidays, notably Christmas, New Year's Day, and Easter.

5. Changing Ways

Over the centuries, the Pueblos moved from cliff dwellings to the surrounding land, keeping many of the old beliefs, even as they adopted new ways.

THE ANASAZI PROSPERED FOR MANY HUNDREDS OF YEARS IN THE LAND OF the sun, achieving a high level of civilization. No one is certain why they abandoned their cliff dwellings and canyons, but by 1300 they had chosen a new way of life in small villages scattered throughout the region. They moved to villages on the Hopi mesas, the Zuñi Plateau, the upper Little Colorado River, and along tributaries of the northern Rio Grande in New Mexico. The Hopi and Zuñi believed the kachinas brought food during a great famine that swept over the land. Over time, the Hopi and Zuñi became more isolated than the eastern Pueblos, who lived along the Rio Grande.

Arrival of the Spanish

It is believed that the Zuñi first encountered Franciscan missionary Marcos de Niza in 1539. A year later the Spanish explorer Francisco Vásquez de Coronado, searching for the legendary Seven Cities of Cíbola, journeyed northward from New Spain (now Mexico) with a party of Spaniards and Indians. Visiting the Hopi, Zuñi, and Rio Grande people, he stole corn and cotton clothing. The party did not find any treasure and returned to Mexico, but the Spanish kept coming back. Greedy for gold, conquistadores took food and supplies from the peaceful inhabitants. If the Pueblos refused to give up their belongings, they were severely punished or murdered. The Spanish were surprised by the high level of civilization, but they did not recognize the Pueblos as equals. The Pueblos became terrified of these invaders

This religious procession of 1921, in which the statue of San José is borne from the Laguna Mission to the plaza shrine, is reminiscent of the time in which the Spanish dominated the Pueblos.

who would not hesitate to kill them, and soon acquiesced to their demands.

The Spanish enslaved the Pueblos or required them to pay heavy taxes in the form of crops and other goods. Missionaries, who viewed the Pueblos as savages, imposed Christianity upon them. Many years later, in 1598, Don Juan de Oñate returned with settlers and their wives, as well as livestock. Viewing the Pueblos as a "conquered people," they created a system called *encomienda* in which they didn't take land, kill people, or destroy their villages. However, the Pueblos were forced to work for the Spanish landlords in payment for food and clothing and to convert to Christianity. This system did not extend to the Hopis and Zuñis who lived on dry stretches to the west. However, the pueblos of the Rio Grande accepted new crops—wheat, chile, and onions—as well as grapes and peaches. They also began to herd sheep, goats, and cattle. Wool replaced cotton as the principal textile. Using horses and burros, they learned new methods of irrigation.

The Pueblos were condemned to a life of servitude in which they labored against their will and were forced to practice an alien religion. Since they couldn't leave the land, they were even more vulnerable to attack from Navajo, Apache, and Comanche warriors. Bands of them raided the carefully tended fields, killed men, and kidnapped women and children, who were sold into slavery in Mexico. The peace-loving Pueblos fought back, but they were already wearied from their warfare with the Spanish conquistadores and the meddlesome priests. They had lived in peace and harmony and knew a better way. If they took a life, they had to be purified in a special ceremony. In earlier days, they would probably have migrated again, but the Spanish now bound them to one place, and these European invaders also possessed the best land.

By 1598 the Spanish had occupied most of Pueblo country, and by 1630 Spanish missions were established in nearly every village. During this time, the Pueblos were also devastated by smallpox, measles, and other diseases brought in by the Spanish. Having no resistance to these illnesses, thousands died.

The Pueblo Revolt

Nearly a hundred years after the Spanish had begun to colonize their homeland, the Pueblos decided they could no longer endure this despotic rule. Allying themselves for the first time in their history, the various Pueblo tribes rose up as one against the settlers. The Navajos joined in the Pueblo Revolt of 1680 as well. People in the villages north of Santa Fe hunted down and killed the Spaniards. The Tewa attacked the fort at Santa Fe, forcing the governor and others to flee to El Paso, Texas.

For twelve years no Spaniard dared to set foot in Pueblo country. Yet this was also a difficult time for the Pueblos. Their crops failed, and with no Spanish forces to repel them, the Navajos and Apaches again raided stores of corn and herds of sheep. Some Pueblo families joined these wandering tribes; whole villages were abandoned. When the Spaniards returned, riding into Santa Fe at the end of the summer of 1692 under a new governor, Diego de

Vargas, they found the Pueblos resigned to their rule. Since that day, descendants of the Spanish soldiers have celebrated their return with an annual march to the Governor's Palace in the plaza at Santa Fe. The Pueblos, however, have never celebrated this day. Most of the people continued to practice their ancient religion, yet the number of villages was reduced from about eighty to thirty. While tending their fields and making pottery, they watched as settlers poured back into the country and took more of their land.

Anglo-American Expansion

When Mexico won independence from Spain in 1821, the Pueblos came under new rulers. Both the Spanish and the Pueblos in New Mexico—then the northern region of Mexico—again suffered from vicious attacks by Navajos and Apaches. The Spanish settlers were too concerned with their own land holdings to worry about the plight of the Pueblos. Then, in 1846, the United States declared war on Mexico and subsequently took all the land that would become the future states of New Mexico, Arizona, Utah, Nevada, and California, as well as parts of Colorado and Wyoming.

The Pueblos now found themselves under the authority of the government of the United States. The Apaches and Navajos were defeated, which at least put an end to the raids and bloodshed. The Pueblos hoped the Americans would treat them more kindly, but it was difficult for the governor of New Mexico, who also

*O*ver time, people adopted many elements of European-style dress from the Spanish and then the Americans who took over their homeland. Today, people continue to blend traditional dress with the latest styles.

served as Indian agent, to convince Washington officials that the Pueblos were peaceful.

Throughout Spanish, Mexican, and American rule, the Pueblos preserved their traditional culture, often superficially adopting religions or governments but secretly holding onto their old ways. The western Pueblos, in particular, resisted these outside influences, while in the eastern villages some Spanish customs and beliefs were adopted. Trappers and traders also introduced new clothing and other goods to the Pueblos, and then railroads cut through Pueblo country, bringing more and cheaper products. Many people abandoned pottery making and weaving, along with traditional styles of dress and housing. European Americans also tended to be prejudiced against people of darker skin. They were afraid of native peoples, including the Pueblos, whom they considered to be primitive savages. Showing no respect for traditional beliefs, they forced children to attend boarding schools hundreds of miles from their homes and families. Here, children learned English, but they were also treated as if they were inferior. They were admonished to abandon the ancient beliefs that had sustained their people for so many generations.

Remaining apart from outside influences, the Hopis rarely allow visitors on their mesas even today. The Zuñis and the eastern Pueblos have also carefully protected the flame of their beliefs. Time-honored ceremonies take place at each of the villages over the course of the seasons and years. Yet the Pueblos have learned to live with modern technology, and the attitudes of outsiders have also changed in recent years. Many people regret the abuse of the Pueblos and have come to appreciate the wisdom of their culture. Pueblo beliefs are rooted deep within their kivas; they are carried in the drumbeats of their dances; they are borne in the dreams of women who make pottery and in the old men who weave at their looms and tell stories to children in the last of the evening light.

Tewa Language

Pueblo culture has been preserved through its languages, which may be classified into four groups: Uto-Aztecan, Keresan, Tanoan, and Zuñi. Tanoan includes the dialects of Towa, Tewa, and Tiwa. The Hopis speak Uto-Aztecan (except the settlement at Hano, where Tewa is spoken) and the Zuñi speak a language—called Zuñi—unrelated to any other. Keresan is spoken by the Pueblos at Acoma, Laguna, Zia, Santa Ana, San Felipe, Santo Domingo, and Cochiti. Tewa is spoken at Tesuque, Pojoaque, Nambe, Santa Clara, San Ildefonso, and San Juan. Tiwa is spoken at Taos, Picuris, Sandia, and Isleta. Tanoan is distantly related to the language of the Kiowa, who were once buffalo hunters on the plains.

Most Pueblo people speak a variation of Keresan or Tanoan, as well as English and often Spanish. Here are some words in Tewa, the most widely spoken of the languages today. They are based primarily on several booklets prepared by the Summer Institute of Linguistics in Santa Ana, California, and on *Tewa Hi?*, a short dictionary of the language.

The sounds for consonants are basically the same as in English. Here are the vowels sounds with equivalent pronunciations in English words:

a	(ah)	as in father
aa	(ah)	as in father, but held longer
ä	(aa)	as in apple
e	(e)	as in they
ee	(e)	as in they, but held longer
u	(oo)	as in flute
uu	(oo)	as in flute, but held longer
i	(ee)	as in machine
ii	(ee)	as in machine, but held longer
o	(oh)	as in open

Some of the following words are especially important to the Tewa. Others are everyday words that may show how much you have in common with Pueblo children.

apple	bee
arrow	su
bag	muu
beans	tuu
bear	kee
bow	su
bread	pava
chicken	dii
cottontail	puu
dog	tse

eagle	tsee
egg	waa
eye	tsii
father	tara
fire	faa
firewood	son
fish	paa
hair	fo
hand	man
heart	pin
leg	po
man	sen
meat	pivi
medicine	woo
mouth	soo
nut	tu
pine	wän
pumpkin	poo
shirt	to
stick	fe
tongue	hän
tree	tee
wagon	te

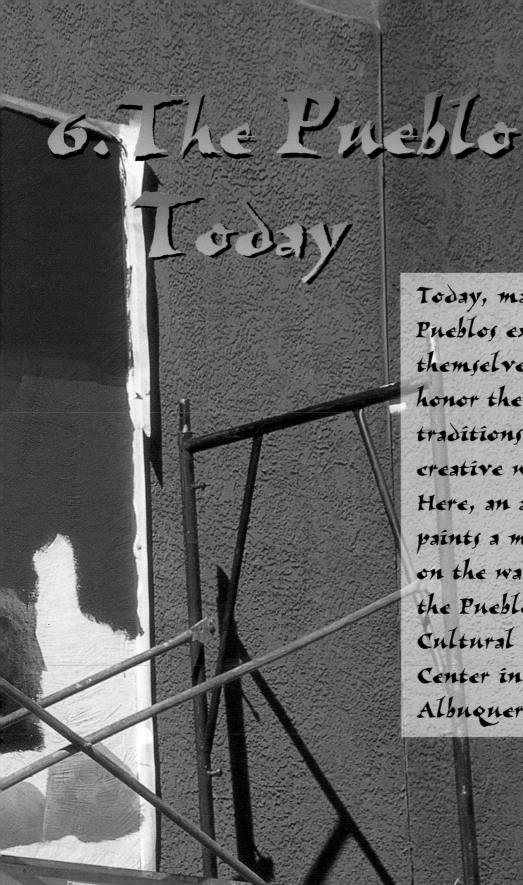

6. The Pueblo Today

Today, many Pueblos express themselves and honor their traditions in creative ways. Here, an artist paints a mural on the wall of the Pueblo Cultural Center in Albuquerque.

AFTER SUFFERING AT THE HANDS OF SPANIARDS, OTHER INDIANS, AND Anglo Americans, the Pueblos of New Mexico live in nineteen villages—some of which were established long before the European discovery of America—along with sheep camps and farm settlements. The Taroan-speaking pueblos along the upper Rio Grande near Santa Fe and Albuquerque include Isleta, Jemez, Nambe, Picuris, San Ildefonso, San Juan, Santa Clara, and Taos; at Cochiti, Santa Ana, Santo Domingo, San Felipe, and Zia, where Keresan languages are spoken. Two slightly westward Keresan pueblos, Acoma, the "Sky City," and Laguna, along with the Zuñi and Hopi pueblos, make up the western villages. Since about 1700 the Zuñi have generally lived in one large village in northwestern New Mexico. The Hopi make their home on or near three mesas in northeastern Arizona; their pueblos include Mishongnovi, Shongopavi (also spelled Shongopovi), Shipaulovi, Sichomovi, and Oraibi along with the Tewa-Hopi village of Hano, founded about 1700 by Tewa-speaking refugees.

Some pueblos, such as the Hopi village of Oraibi, have developed a split between conservative and progressive members. The conflict has led to the decline of the pueblo as members move away to other settlements. Geography and culture still influence Pueblo life. Living in relative isolation on their own reservation, the Hopi have their own schools and hospitals, staffed with their own doctors and nurses. Since the Indian Reorganization Act of 1934 they have chosen their own leaders and have governed themselves. The Zuñi, who live near Gallup, New Mexico, and have easy access to highways and railroads, have interacted more

Many Pueblos, like this young man at San Ildefonso Pueblo, continue to live in adobe homes in their villages. They earn a living by making and selling pottery, jewelry, and other handicrafts to visitors.

with the Pueblos living along the Rio Grande. Today, there are eight pueblos north of Santa Fe—Taos being the farthest north— and eleven south of Santa Fe. None of them are as isolated as in the days of travel over bumpy dirt roads.

Today, many people commute to larger cities to work, but return to their pueblos at night. Others come home several times a year to attend religious ceremonies and to visit their families.

Land remains a bitter question among many Pueblos. All the Pueblos had their land granted to them by Spain. The land is the actual property of the villages—a right affirmed by the United States Congress in 1848. The Pueblos are among the few Indian nations that hold title to the land instead of living on land set aside or "reserved" for them by the United States. Still, land was taken from the Pueblos, some of which has since been returned. The people themselves have bought back some of their ancestral homelands. Other parcels have been placed in public domain, to be used for grazing and camping by all people. A few areas, such as the Blue Lake of Taos, have been reserved as sacred places. Today, each pueblo manages its own land.

Pueblo livelihood is still based on growing crops and raising livestock, along with the sale of creative work. The men of each village cooperatively tend fields of corn, beans, cotton, melons, squash, and chili peppers. Men also weave, build houses, and undertake ceremonies while the women prepare meals, care for the children, make baskets and pottery, and carry water. Women help with gardening and building the houses, just as they once participated in communal hunts. Taos ranchers herd cattle in the high country, as do the people living near the green pastures of the Rio Grande at Isleta. In their dry country the Zuñi have become sheepherders. Many people raise corn and other crops to be sold as well as to feed themselves. Those who have left their villages in search of work visit frequently for celebrations to keep in touch with the social and religious values of their people. Others have moved back to rediscover the roots of their culture.

The pueblos of today remain solid, square buildings of adobe bricks or stone set in clay and mortar, with thick flat roofs and square rooms. Some, notably Taos, are terraced in multistories with wooden ladders leaning on the walls, but there are no longer trapdoors in the roofs. Modern buildings have hinged doors and glass windows, along with electricity and plumbing. Rooms may be added as needed, and everyone in the village often lives in a single complex. Each pueblo has one or more kivas.

In June, July, and August there are feasts and festivals at the pueblos, and many are open to visitors who wish to see the traditional dances. Some, such as the Acoma Pueblo, offer tours.

Although the pueblos retain many similar cultural elements, each is unique with distinctive languages and techniques for making baskets, pottery, and jewelry. Many of the old crafts, especially pottery and jewelry making, are being revived. Like their Anasazi ancestors, women still make striking pottery and jewelry. They have refined the blend of turquoise and silver into a high form of art. Pottery is characterized by striking decoration and shapes unmatched among Native Americans. The high quality of Pueblo pottery is recognized throughout the world. The exquisite work of potters such as Maria Martinez is prized by museums and art collectors. During the middle years of the twentieth century, the distinguished Acoma potter Lucy M. Lewis introduced black-on-white designs inspired by Anasazi bowls that had been made hundreds of years earlier.

Men continue to be skilled weavers, making cotton and woolen clothing and fine woolen blankets. The Pueblos have also proved to be particularly gifted painters.

A new pride has risen from deep within the hearts and souls of the Pueblos. To save their way of life many have withdrawn to the secrecy of their religious customs and emphasized the details of their traditional dress to set themselves apart from the overwhelming influence of modern technology and materialism. This rekindling has given them a renewed identity as a native people with a rich heritage and a bright future.

*E*ntitled Pueblo Moonlight, *this woodcut made by Howard Cook in 1927 expressively illustrates the distinctive rectangular shape of multi-storied pueblos, which are still home to many people.*

More About

the Pueblo

Time Line

10,000 B.C. First native peoples come to live in the American Southwest

A.D. 900s Early Pueblo peoples are trading for seashells, parrot feathers, and other items. There is also evidence of the bow and arrow, pottery, masonry, and other cultural development

950–1000 Pueblos begin to migrate to the Rio Grande valley in present-day New Mexico

1050–1300 Anasazi culture reaches the height of its development

1275–1300 In a mass migration of Anasazi people the Four Corners area is vacated

1400 Athabascan-speaking people (Apaches and Navajos) arrive in the Southwest

1500s Spanish explorers wander the Southwest in search of gold

1540 Francisco Vásquez de Coronado encounters the Pueblos

1581 A group of Spanish missionaries returns to the Southwest to attempt to bring the Pueblos under their influence

1598 Don Juan de Oñate takes control of New Mexico as a colony; Franciscan missionaries are assigned to seven pueblos

1598–1680 Spanish missionaries attempt to Christianize the Pueblos and bring them under the control of religious authorities

1610 Spain formally claims all the Southwest, including Pueblo land, as a colony in the New World

1680 In the massive Pueblo Revolt, the Pueblos and other Native Americans drive the Spanish from the Four Corners area

1692 The Spanish retake the region, except for Hopi lands

1811 Spain grants the Pueblos full rights as Spanish citizens and eliminates special protection for Pueblo lands

1821 Mexico wins independence from Spain and takes control of New Mexico, including Pueblo lands

1822 The Santa Fe Trail is blazed, bringing traders and American goods to the Pueblo people

1824 The United States establishes the Bureau of Indian Affairs

1848 The Mexican War concludes with the Treaty of Guadalupe Hidalgo; Mexico cedes the Southwest to the United States

1850 The United States officially claims New Mexico as a territory, granting no legal protection to Pueblo lands

1864–1868 Navajos are imprisoned at Fort Sumner (Bosque Redondo), bringing an end to raids on Pueblo lands

1880s Railroads reach New Mexico and Arizona, bringing traders, settlers, and tourists fascinated by Pueblo culture

1908 President Theodore Roosevelt authorizes the Blue Lake region to become part of Carson National Forest in New Mexico

1912 New Mexico becomes the forty-seventh state in the Union

1924 The U.S. Congress approves the Pueblo Lands Act; Native Americans born in the United States, including Pueblos, are declared citizens

1934 The Indian Reorganization Act recognizes tribal governments

1950s Pueblos and other native peoples successfully resist a federal relocation program intended to integrate them into urban society

1970 President Richard Nixon approves the return of 48,000 acres of the Blue Lake region of Carson National Forest to the Taos Pueblos

1980 Celebration of the three hundredth anniversary of the Pueblo Revolt

Notable People

Thomas Banyacya Sr., Hopi (about 1910–   ), Pueblo activist and leader, was born on the Hopi Reservation at New Oraibi. He became renowned in 1948 when elders selected him as one of four men to be

Thomas Banyacya Sr.

their "tongue and ears" in warning the white world of ancient prophecies. The Hopi predicted an enormous "gourdful of ashes," which materialized when the first atomic bomb was detonated in 1945. The Hopi warned that there would be a nuclear holocaust if people did not change their destructive ways. Banyacya has become a prominent advocate in the American Southwest for traditional ways. He strongly protested the strip-mining of Black Mesa and the forced relocation of 10,000 Navajos on land adjacent to the Hopi Reservation. He continues to protest the activities of mining companies and tribal governments to this day.

Helen Quintana Cordero, Cochiti (1915–   ), sculptor, lives in Cochiti, New Mexico, and is an accomplished sculptor of clay figurines. For thousands of years, Native Americans in the Southwest made clay figures, but the art was nearly lost by the late 1800s. In the 1950s, after briefly experimenting with leather and bead crafts, Helen began to make clay figures. She revived the craft, notably the Singing Mother Doll, and created her own popular Storyteller Doll. In 1964, she won first, second, and third place prizes at the New Mexico State Fair. She has since received many national and international honors for her work, and she is considered the foremost maker of these distinctive clay figures today.

Crescensio Martinez (Te E), San Ildefonso Pueblo (about 1890–1918), noted painter, was born and lived his entire life at San Ildefonso. He first painted pottery, then turned to watercolors around 1910. Edgar Lee Hewett of the Museum of New Mexico gave paper and watercolors to Martinez after seeing him drawing on cardboard. Martinez was commissioned to do paintings depicting the dances of the summer and winter ceremonies for the museum collection. Martinez also painted a series of watercolors for the School of American Research, and his work was featured at the Society of Independent Artists in New York City and at the American Museum of Natural History. Sadly, his life was cut short by pneumonia in 1918 during an influenza epidemic. Despite his brief career, his portrayals of ceremonial life drew the admiration of many and inspired other Pueblo artists in Santa Fe.

Julian Martinez (Pocano), San Ildefonso Pueblo (about 1883–1943), potter and painter, was born at San Ildefonso Pueblo in the 1880s. He married Maria Montoya in 1904 and earned a living as a farmer and painter. Over the years, he became more accomplished as a painter and was asked to create artwork for several government buildings in the region. He and Maria moved back to San Ildefonso and experimented with pottery making, rediscovering a way of making a satiny black finish. Using this special technique, Julian and his well-known wife enjoyed a great deal of success in making pottery, and over the course of their lives the couple greatly influenced the growth of ceramic art in the Southwest.

Julian Martinez

Maria Montoya Martinez

Maria Montoya Martinez, San Ildefonso Pueblo (1887–1980), a well-known potter, first demonstrated her pottery making at the St. Louis world's fair in 1904—the first of three world's fairs in which she would exhibit fine pottery. Her husband, Julian, worked at an excavation of Pueblo ruins in 1907. Edgar Hewett, who was directing the excavation, asked Maria if she could create pottery similar to the thin, polished potsherds found at the site. After many experiments, she was able to match the ancient pottery.

She and Julian developed a unique way of making black-on-black pottery in 1919, and in 1923 Maria Martinez began to sign her pottery which was now highly prized by collectors. After the death of her husband, Maria began to make pottery with her daughter-in-law and then with her son Tony, who is known as Popovi Da. Maria Martinez received many awards and honors for her work. She was invited to the White House four times.

Tony Martinez (Popovi Da), San Ildefonso Pueblo (1923–1971), a highly regarded artist, was the eldest son of the gifted artists Julian and Maria Martinez. He excelled in art at the Santa Fe Indian School from which he graduated in 1939. Encouraged by his parents, he first took up painting, but when his father died in 1943 he began to make lovely pottery with his mother. After serving in the army during World War II, he opened a studio in San Ildefonso plaza in 1948 and changed his name to Popovi Da, which means "Red Fox." He and his mother continued to experiment with designs and a unique black and sienna matte pottery. He also began to make impressive silver jewelry. He represented Pueblo art at many national and international conferences.

Nampeyo (Tcu-Mana, Nampayu, Nampayo), Hopi-Tewa (about 1859–1942), a potter, was born at Hano, Arizona. As she grew up, Nampeyo, whose name means "Snake Girl" or "Snake That Does Not Bite," watched her grandmother make water pots. In 1881, she began to revive traditional Hopi pottery shapes and designs. Visiting ancient Anasazi sites, she discovered many other styles of pottery, and by the end of the century she was recognized as a major Pueblo artist. She sold her pottery in the lobby of the Grand Canyon Lodge operated by the Fred Harvey Company, which owned a chain of hotels, and Harvey helped her to win international acclaim. Her work was also acquired by the Smithsonian Institution. Through her talent and hard work, Hopi pottery came to be recognized as an art form.

Alfonso Ortiz, Tewa (1939–1997), a noted anthropologist, was born at San Juan, the largest of the six remaining Tewa pueblos. An excellent student, he won a National Merit Scholarship and earned a bachelor's degree at the University of New Mexico in 1961. Receiving his master's and doctoral degrees at the University of Chicago, he taught at Princeton University before returning home in 1974 to become a professor at the University of New Mexico.

As a member of the San Juan Pueblo, Dr. Ortiz was able to penetrate the mysteries of ritual and religion. He wrote a landmark book of anthropology entitled *The Tewa World: Space, Time, Being, and Becoming in Pueblo Society*, which was published in 1969. He edited several other books on American Indian anthropology. He received a Guggenheim fellowship in 1975 and he became a MacArthur Fellow in 1982.

Simon Ortiz, Acoma Pueblo (1941–   ), a poet and author, was born in Albuquerque, New Mexico. Raised at Acoma Pueblo, he developed a deep appreciation for the strength of words from his father. During the 1960s, he attended various colleges, including the University of New Mexico and the University of Iowa. Strongly influenced by N. Scott

Momaday, James Welch, and other Native American writers, he became an accomplished poet. Intended to be both read and spoken, his songs and poems emphasize a sense of place through which Native Americans may find their identity. His most notable works of poetry are *Going for the Rain* (1976) and *Fight Back: For the Sake of the People* (1980).

Tonita Peña

Tonita Peña (Quah Ah), San Ildefonso Pueblo (1895–1949), a well-known painter, was born into an artistic family. Educated at San Ildefonso Pueblo and St. Catherine's School in nearby Santa Fe, by age twenty-one, Peña was a successful painter who sold her works throughout the Southwest. Despite her lack of formal training, she was encouraged to develop her own innovative style. Her artwork has appeared in numerous publications and has been collected by many museums. When she died in 1949 she was considered the "Grand Old Lady of Pueblo Art."

Popé, Tewa (about 1633–1690), an influential religious leader, organized a resistance movement against the Spanish in the 1600s. After being imprisoned by the Spanish, he went to Taos Pueblo and instigated a rebellion. Other Hopi and Pueblo leaders joined him. On August 10, 1680, they attacked Spanish outposts and haciendas near the Rio Grande. A force of five hundred warriors then stormed Santa Fe, cutting off the water supply and driving the Spanish out of the city. Popé ordered that all traces of the Spanish be eliminated. Yet Popé became as dictatorial as the Spanish, adopting their luxuries and executing his enemies. A drought, along with raids by Utes and Apaches led to discontent among the people and his eventual overthrow. He later regained power, but when he died around 1690 the Pueblos were in disarray, and the Spanish regained control in 1692.

Ben Quintana (Ha-A-Tee), Cochiti Pueblo (about 1925–1944), a well-known painter, was taught as a young boy by Tonita Peña, an artist at Cochiti, and later by Po-tsunu, another highly regarded artist. In 1940, at about age fifteen, Quintana won the New Mexico State Coronado Quadricentennial Competition. Two years later, in 1942, one of his posters won first prize in a competition sponsored by *American* magazine. He also painted murals for schools during these years. He served in the armed forces during World War II and was killed in action in the Philippines on November 9, 1944. His paintings have since been acquired by museums and collectors around the world.

Wendy Rose, Hopi, Chowchilla, and Miwok (1948–   ), poet, author, and activist, was born in Oakland, California, and raised in the San Francisco Bay Area. While she was an anthropology student at the University of California at Berkeley she married Arthur Murata. After she completed her master's degree in 1978 she taught in the Native American and Ethnic Studies programs at Berkeley and later at Fresno State University. From 1984 to the present, she has been the coordinator of the American Indian Studies Program at Fresno City College. Her most important works are *Hopi Roadrunner Dancing*; *Long Division: A Tribal History*; and *Builder Kachina: A Home-Going Cycle*.

Leslie Marmon Silko, Laguna Pueblo (1948–   ), poet and writer, was born in Albuquerque, New Mexico, and raised on the Laguna Reservation. As she grew up, she was immersed in Keres and Laguna culture. She attended the University of New Mexico where she graduated magna cum laude in 1969. She has taught at Navajo Community College, the University of New Mexico, and the University of Arizona.

Leslie Marmon Silko

Dedicating herself to writing poetry and fiction, she wrote her first novel, *Ceremony*, which, along with *Storyteller*, was published in 1981. She received a prestigious MacArthur Foundation fellowship, which allowed her time to complete a novel entitled *Almanac of the Dead*, published in 1991. Much of Silko's work reflects the storytelling tradition of Native American peoples.

Louis Tawanima, Hopi (about 1879–1969), an Olympic athlete, was born at Shongopovi, Second Mesa, on the Hopi Reservation in Arizona. Coached by football legend Glenn S. "Pop" Warner, he and Jim Thorpe competed in numerous track-and-field events at the Carlisle Indian School. In the 1908 Olympics held in London, Tawanima ran in the marathon. In the 1912 Olympics in Stockholm, Sweden, he won the silver medal in the 10,000-meter run. That same year, he also won the twelve-mile derby in New York City. He was inducted into the Arizona Hall of Fame in 1957. In 1969, blind in old age, he fell to his death from a mesa while walking home along a narrow path.

Youkioma, Hopi (about 1880–1929), was born and raised in Old Oraibi, Third Mesa, on the Pueblo Reservation in Arizona. Youkioma became a leader of a conservative group that wished to save traditional Hopi culture. He subsequently led a group away to establish Hotevilla (New Oraibi), a village of about four hundred people. White authorities jailed Youkioma on several occasions after this and sent him to the Carlisle Indian School in Pennsylvania. In 1911, Youkioma and Lawshe, the Hopi Indian agent, traveled to Washington, D.C., to lobby for Hopi independence. He lived the rest of his life in Hotevilla.

Glossary

adobe Clay applied like plaster as a building material. Sometimes mixed with grass or straw to strengthen the bond.

Anasazi A Hopi word meaning "the ancient ones," which refers to the early Pueblos.

cliff dwelling An ancient home of multistoried adobe or stone, built on a cliff or high terrace.

conquistadores Spanish soldiers who brutally subjugated native peoples of Central and South America as well as the American Southwest.

kachina The group of over 250 sacred beings believed to be the spirits of plants, animals, people, and places.

kiva An underground chamber for religious celebrations, usually located in the center of the village.

mano A flat, rectangular stone held in the hand and scraped back and forth against a metate to make cornmeal.

mesa A hill or mountain with steep sides and a flat top like a table.

metate A flat, rectangular stone used for grinding corn into meal.

mission An adobe church where people came together to worship, used by priests to teach about Christianity.

piki Pueblo bread made of paper-thin layers of cornmeal batter quickly cooked on a hot flat stone.

pit house An early Anasazi home built partly underground.

plaza The central public area in a village or town where people gathered for public events, similar to a town square.

pueblo The Spanish word for village; when capitalized it is used to identify several different Native American peoples of the Southwest.

sipapu The word for navel, referring to the sacred place beneath the earth from which all life originated; the opening of the kiva today.

Further Information

Readings

Over the years many fine books have been written about the Pueblos. Among them, the following titles were very helpful in researching and writing *The Pueblo*.

"Coyote and Cottontail" was adapted from a longer version of the story called "The Race of the Tails," collected by Charles F. Lummis and published in *Pueblo Indian Folk-Stories*. "The Emergence Story" is adapted from "The Tewa Emergence Legend," by Tito Naranjo, published in *Native Americans of the Southwest*. The poems in *The Pueblo* were drawn from *Songs of the Tewa*, by Herbert Joseph Spinden.

Cordell, Linda S. *Ancient Pueblo Peoples*. Washington, D.C.: Smithsonian Books, 1994.

Curtis, Edward S. *The North American Indian: Being a Series of Volumes Picturing and Describing the Indians of the United States and Alaska*. New York: Johnson Reprint Corp., 1970.

Erdoes, Richard. *Native Americans: The Pueblos*. New York: Sterling Publishing.

——. *The Rain Dance People: The Pueblo Indians, Their Past and Present*. New York: Alfred A. Knopf, 1976.

Hausman, Gerald. *Turtle Dream: Collected Stories from the Hopi, Navajo, Pueblo, and Havasupai People*. Santa Fe: Mariposa Publishing, 1989.

Hughes, Phyllis. *Pueblo Indian Cookbook*. Santa Fe: Museum of New Mexico Press, 1972.

Johansen, Bruce E. and Grinde, Donald A. Jr. *The Encyclopedia of Native American Biography*. New York: Henry Holt, 1997.

Lummis, Charles F. *Pueblo Indian Folk-Stories*. Lincoln, Neb.: University of Nebraska Press, 1992.

Malinowski, Sharon. *Notable Native Americans*. Detroit: Gale Research, 1995.

Marriott, Alice. *Indians of the Four Corners: A Book About the Anasazi Indians and Their Modern Descendants*. New York: Thomas Y. Crowell, 1952.

Ortiz, Alfonso. *Handbook of North American Indians*. Volume 9, Southwest. Washington, D. C.: Smithsonian Institution, 1979.

Reed, Evelyn Dahl. *Coyote Tales from the Indian Pueblos*. Santa Fe: Sunstone Press, 1998.

Roediger, Virginia More. *Ceremonial Costumes of the Pueblo Indians: Their Evolution, Education, Fabrication, and Significance in the Prayer Drama*. Berkeley: University of California Press, 1941.

Sando, Joe S. *The Pueblo Indians*. San Francisco: The Indian Historical Press, 1976.

———. *Pueblo Nations: Cultural Identity Through Centuries of Change*. Santa Fe: Clear Light Publishers, 1997.

———. *Pueblo Nations: Eight Centuries of Pueblo Indian History*. Santa Fe: Clear Light Publishers, 1992.

Shanks, Ralph C., and Shanks, Lisa Woo. *The North American Indian Travel Guide*. Petaluma, Calif.: Costano Books, 1993.

Underhill, Ruth. *Life in the Pueblos*. Santa Fe: Ancient City Press, 1991.

Warren, Scott. *Cities in the Sand: The Ancient Civilizations of the Southwest*. San Francisco: Chronicle Books, 1992.

Wyckoff, Lydia L. *Visions and Voices: Native American Painting from the Philbrook Museum of Art*. Tulsa, Okla.:The Philbrook Museum of Art, 1994.

Young people who wish to learn more about the Pueblo peoples will enjoy these fine books for children:

Arnold, Caroline. *The Ancient Cliff Dwellers of Mesa Verde*. New York: Clarion Books, 1992.

Ayer, Eleanor H. *The Anasazi*. New York: Walker, 1993.

Bird, E. J. *The Rainmakers*. Minneapolis: Carolrhoda Books, 1993

Burby, Liza N. *The Pueblo Indians*. New York: Chelsea Juniors, 1994.

Cory, Steven. *Pueblo Indian*. Minneapolis: Lerner Publications, 1996.

D'Apice, Mary. *The Pueblo*. Vero Beach, Fla.: Rourke Publications, 1990.

Fisher, Leonard Everett. *Anasazi*. New York: Atheneum Books for Young Readers, 1997.

Hoyt-Goldsmith, Diane. *Pueblo Storyteller*. New York: Holiday House, 1991.

Hubbard-Brown, Janet. *A History Mystery: The Disappearance of the Anasazi*. New York: Avon Books, 1992.

James, J. Alison. *Sing for a Gentle Rain*. New York: Atheneum, 1990.

Keegan, Marcia. *Pueblo Boy: Growing Up in Two Worlds*. New York: Cobblehill Books, 1991.

Mott, Evelyn. *Dancing Rainbows: A Pueblo Boy's Story*. New York: Cobblehill Books, 1996.

Paul, Sherry. *Ancient Skyscrapers: The Native American Pueblos*. New York: Contemporary Perspectives, 1978.

Peterson, David. *The Anasazi*. Chicago: Children's Press, 1991.

Powell, Suzanne. *The Pueblos*. New York: Franklin Watts, 1993.

Vallo, Lawrence Jonathan. *Tales of a Pueblo Boy*. Santa Fe: Sunstone Press, 1987.

Pueblo Websites

Over the past few years, Native Americans have established themselves on the Internet. Here are some of the best and most interesting websites to visit for more information about the Pueblo people.

Anasazi Heritage Center
http://www.co.blm.gov/ahc/hmepge.htm

Bandelier National Monument
http://www.nps.gov/band

Canyon de Chelly National Monument
http://www.nps.gov/cach

Chaco Culture National Historical Park
http://www.nps.gov/chcu

Hopi Cultural Center
http://www.psv.com/hopi.html

Anasazi Ruins

Anasazi villages are now preserved as national parks, historic sites, or national monuments. Every year, many people visit these old pueblos. Mesa Verde is one of the best-known sites, partly because of the fine condition of the buildings. Located in southwestern Colorado, it covers eighty square miles. The most famous structure located there is the Cliff Palace—the largest cliff dwelling in the United States. Chaco Canyon in New Mexico includes a large, four-story apartment that once housed around six hundred people. Protected by the government since 1907, Pueblo Bonito may have been the principal center of Anasazi culture because of its location and expansive system of roadways. Navajo National Monument, established in Kayenta, Arizona, in 1909, features Betatakin, Keet Seel, and Inscription House, some of the largest early Pueblo ruins. (Inscription House itself has sixty-five rooms.) Canyon de Chelly in Chinle, Arizona, is the site of several ruins, including the famous White House Ruin.

Pueblo Villages Today

Despite hundreds of years of suffering from European invasions, warfare with other Native American tribes, and dominance by the culture and economy of Anglo Americans, the Pueblo people have maintained their communities, some of which have been continuously inhabited for hundreds of years. Embracing an ancient, private, and deeply religious way of life, the Pueblos carry on a proud heritage.

New Mexico Pueblos

Acoma Pueblo
P. O. Box 309
Acomita, NM 87034
(505) 552-6604

Cochiti Pueblo
P. O. Box 70
Cochiti, NM 87041
(505) 465-2244

Isleta Pueblo
P. O. Box 317
Isleta, NM 87022
(505) 869-3111 or
(505) 869-6333

Jemez Pueblo
P. O. Box 100
Jemez, NM 87024
(505) 834-7359

Laguna Pueblo
P. O. Box 194
Laguna, NM 87026
(505) 552-6654

Nambe Pueblo
Route 1, P. O. Box 117 BB
Santa Fe, NM 87501
(505) 455-7752
or (505) 455-7905

Picuris Pueblo
P. O. Box 127
Peñasco, NM 87553
(505) 587-2519

Pojoaque Pueblo
Route 1, P. O. Box 71
Santa Fe, NM 87501
(505) 455-2278
or (505) 455-2279
Fax (505) 455-2950

Sandia Pueblo
P. O. Box 6008
Bernalillo, NM 87004
(505) 867-3317

San Felipe Pueblo
P. O. Box A
San Felipe Pueblo,
NM 87001
(505) 867-3381

San Ildefonso Pueblo
Route 5, P. O. Box 315 A
Santa Fe, NM 87501
(505) 455-2273

San Juan Pueblo
P. O. Box 1099
San Juan Pueblo,
NM 87566
(505) 852-4400
or (505) 852-4210

Santa Ana Pueblo
P. O. Box 37
Bernalillo, NM 87004
(505) 867-3301

Santa Clara Pueblo
P. O. Box 580
Española, NM 87532
(505) 753-7326
or (505) 753-7330

Santo Domingo Pueblo
P. O. Box 99
Santo Domingo Pueblo,
NM 87052
(505) 465-2214

Taos Pueblo
P. O. Box 1846
Taos, NM 87571
(505) 758-9593
Fax (505) 758-8831

Tesuque Pueblo
Route 11, P. O. Box 1
Santa Fe, NM 87501
(505) 983-2667

Zia Pueblo
General Delivery
San Ysidro, NM 87053
(505) 867-3304

Zuñi Pueblo
P. O. Box 339
Zuñi, NM 87327
(505)

Index

Page numbers for illustrations are in **boldface**.

Raymond Bial

HAS PUBLISHED OVER THIRTY CRITICALLY ACCLAIMED BOOKS OF PHOTOGRAPHS for children and adults. His photo-essays for children include *Corn Belt Harvest, Amish Home, Frontier Home, Shaker Home, The Underground Railroad, Portrait of a Farm Family, With Needle and Thread: A Book About Quilts, Mist Over the Mountains: Appalachia and Its People, Cajun Home,* and *Where Lincoln Walked.*

He is currently immersed in writing *Lifeways,* a series of books about Native Americans. As with his other work, Bial's deep feelings for his subjects is evident in both the text and illustrations. He travels to tribal cultural centers, photographing homes, artifacts, and surroundings and learning firsthand about the national lifeways of each of these peoples.

A full-time library director at a small college in Champaign, Illinois, he lives with his wife and three children in nearby Urbana.